Managing Programs for Learning Outside the Classroom

Patricia Senn Breivik, *Editor*
University of Colorado, Denver

NEW DIRECTIONS FOR HIGHER EDUCATION
MARTIN KRAMER, *Editor-in-Chief*
University of California, Berkeley

Number 56, Winter 1986

Paperback sourcebooks in
The Jossey-Bass Higher Education Series

Jossey-Bass Inc., Publishers
San Francisco • London

Patricia Senn Breivik (ed.).
Managing Programs for Learning Outside the Classroom.
New Directions for Higher Education, no. 56.
Volume XIV, number 4.
San Francisco: Jossey-Bass, 1986.

New Directions for Higher Education
Martin Kramer, *Editor-in-Chief*

Copyright © 1986 by Jossey-Bass Inc., Publishers
and
Jossey-Bass Limited

Copyright under International, Pan American, and Universal
Copyright Conventions. All rights reserved. No part of
this issue may be reproduced in any form—except for brief
quotation (not to exceed 500 words) in a review or professional
work—without permission in writing from the publishers.

New Directions for Higher Education is published quarterly
by Jossey-Bass Inc., Publishers (publication number USPS
990-880). *New Directions* is numbered sequentially—please
order extra copies by sequential number. The volume and issue
numbers above are included for the convenience of libraries.
Second-class postage paid at San Francisco, California, and at
additional mailing offices. POSTMASTER: Send address changes to
Jossey-Bass Inc., Publishers, 433 California Street, San Francisco,
California 94104.

Editorial correspondence should be sent to the Editor-in-Chief,
Martin Kramer, 2807 Shasta Road, Berkeley, California 94708.

Library of Congress Catalog Card Number 85-644752

International Standard Serial Number ISSN 0271-0560

International Standard Book Number ISBN 1-55542-985-8

Cover art by WILLI BAUM

Manufactured in the United States of America

Ordering Information

The paperback sourcebooks listed below are published quarterly and can be ordered either by subscription or single-copy.

Subscriptions cost $40.00 per year for institutions, agencies, and libraries. Individuals can subscribe at the special rate of $30.00 per year *if payment is by personal check*. (Note that the full rate of $40.00 applies if payment is by institutional check, even if the subscription is designated for an individual.) Standing orders are accepted.

Single copies are available at $9.95 when payment accompanies order, and *all single-copy orders under $25.00 must include payment*. (California, New Jersey, New York, and Washington, D.C., residents please include appropriate sales tax.) For billed orders, cost per copy is $9.95 plus postage and handling. (Prices subject to change without notice.)

Bulk orders (ten or more copies) of any individual sourcebook are available at the following discounted prices: 10-49 copies, $8.95 each; 50-100 copies, $7.96 each; over 100 copies, *inquire*. Sales tax and postage and handling charges apply as for single copy orders.

Please note that these prices are for the academic year 1986-1987 and are subject to change without prior notice. Also, some titles may be out of print and therefore not available for sale.

To ensure correct and prompt delivery, all orders must give either the *name of an individual* or an *official purchase order number. Please submit your order as follows:*

    Subscriptions: specify series and year subscription is to begin.
    Single Copies: specify sourcebook code (such as, HE1) and first two words of title.

Mail orders for United States and Possessions, Latin America, Canada, Japan, Australia, and New Zealand to:
    Jossey-Bass Inc., Publishers
    433 California Street
    San Francisco, California 94104

Mail orders for all other parts of the world to:
    Jossey-Bass Limited
    28 Banner Street
    London EC1Y 8QE

New Directions for Higher Education Series
Martin Kramer, *Editor-in-Chief*

HE1   *Facilitating Faculty Development*, Mervin Freedman
HE2   *Strategies for Budgeting*, George Kaludis
HE3   *Services for Students*, Joseph Katz

HE4 *Evaluating Learning and Teaching,* C. Robert Pace
HE5 *Encountering the Unionized University,* Jack H. Schuster
HE6 *Implementing Field Experience Education,* John Duley
HE7 *Avoiding Conflict in Faculty Personnel Practices,* Richard Peairs
HE8 *Improving Statewide Planning,* James L. Wattenbarger, Louis W. Bender
HE9 *Planning the Future of the Undergraduate College,* Donald G. Trites
HE10 *Individualizing Education by Learning Contracts,* Neal R. Berte
HE11 *Meeting Women's New Educational Needs,* Clare Rose
HE12 *Strategies for Significant Survival,* Clifford T. Stewart, Thomas R. Harvey
HE13 *Promoting Consumer Protection for Students,* Joan S. Stark
HE14 *Expanding Recurrent and Nonformal Education,* David Harman
HE15 *A Comprehensive Approach to Institutional Development,* William Bergquist, William Shoemaker
HE16 *Improving Educational Outcomes,* Oscar Lenning
HE17 *Renewing and Evaluating Teaching,* John A. Centra
HE18 *Redefining Service, Research, and Teaching,* Warren Bryan Martin
HE19 *Managing Turbulence and Change,* John D. Millett
HE20 *Increasing Basic Skills by Developmental Studies,* John E. Roueche
HE21 *Marketing Higher Education,* David W. Barton, Jr.
HE22 *Developing and Evaluating Administrative Leadership,* Charles F. Fisher
HE23 *Admitting and Assisting Students After Bakke,* Alexander W. Astin, Bruce Fuller, Kenneth C. Green
HE24 *Institutional Renewal Through the Improvement of Teaching,* Jerry G. Gaff
HE25 *Assuring Access for the Handicapped,* Martha Ross Redden
HE26 *Assessing Financial Health,* Carol Frances, Sharon L. Coldren
HE27 *Building Bridges to the Public,* Louis T. Benezet, Frances W. Magnusson
HE28 *Preparing for the New Decade,* Larry W. Jones, Franz A. Nowotny
HE29 *Educating Learners of All Ages,* Elinor Greenberg, Kathleen M. O'Donnell, William Bergquist
HE30 *Managing Facilities More Effectively,* Harvey H. Kaiser
HE31 *Rethinking College Responsibilities for Values,* Mary Louise McBee
HE32 *Resolving Conflict in Higher Education,* Jane E. McCarthy
HE33 *Professional Ethics in University Administration,* Ronald H. Stein, M. Carlota Baca
HE34 *New Approaches to Energy Conservation,* Sidney G. Tickton
HE35 *Management Science Applications to Academic Administration,* James A. Wilson
HE36 *Academic Leaders as Managers,* Robert H. Atwell, Madeleine F. Green
HE37 *Designing Academic Program Reviews,* Richard F. Wilson
HE38 *Successful Responses to Financial Difficulties,* Carol Frances
HE39 *Priorities for Academic Libraries,* Thomas J. Galvin, Beverly P. Lynch
HE40 *Meeting Student Aid Needs in a Period of Retrenchment,* Martin Kramer
HE41 *Issues in Faculty Personnel Policies,* Jon W. Fuller
HE42 *Management Techniques for Small and Specialized Institutions,* Andrew J. Falender, John C. Merson
HE43 *Meeting the New Demand for Standards,* Jonathan R. Warren
HE44 *The Expanding Role of Telecommunications in Higher Education,* Pamela J. Tate, Marilyn Kressel
HE45 *Women in Higher Education Administration,* Adrian Tinsley, Cynthia Secor, Sheila Kaplan

HE46 *Keeping Graduate Programs Responsive to National Needs,*
       Michael J. Pelczar, Jr., Lewis C. Solmon
HE47 *Leadership Roles of Chief Academic Officers,* David G. Brown
HE48 *Financial Incentives for Academic Quality,* John Folger
HE49 *Leadership and Institutional Renewal,* Ralph M. Davis
HE50 *Applying Corporate Management Strategies,* Roger J. Flecher
HE51 *Incentive for Faculty Vitality,* Roger G. Baldwin
HE52 *Making the Budget Process Work,* David J. Berg, Gerald M. Skogley
HE53 *Managing College Enrollments,* Don Hossler
HE54 *Institutional Revival: Case Histories,* Douglas W. Steeples
HE55 *Crisis Management in Higher Education,* Hal Hoverland, Pat McInturff,
       C. E. Tapie Rohm, Jr.

Contents

Editor's Notes   1
Patricia Senn Breivik

1. Implementing Nonclassroom Learning: Management Considerations   7
Jerome F. Wartgow
Managers must be prepared to deal with basic issues of symbolism and institutional culture before nonclassroom learning can be effectively implemented.

2. Self-Paced Instruction   17
Michael P. Stowers, Martin Tessmer
Self-paced instruction can be particularly attractive to nontraditional students, but to be most effective, student support systems will need to be more flexible.

3. Telecourses: More Than Meets the Eye   27
Leslie N. Purdy
With the increased availability of quality courses, administrators should consider how telecourses might help their institutions reach new students.

4. Interactive Television   37
Michael Bisesi, B. Dell Felder
Universities can offer opportunities for workers in high-technology fields to gain state-of-the-art information and skills without traveling to campus.

5. Library-Based Learning in an Information Society   47
Patricia Senn Breivik
New approaches to quality issues regarding active learning can be achieved through more imaginative use of campus libraries. Benefits can be extended to faculty development activities and community relations.

6. Field Experience, Practicums, and Internships   57
Virginia Witucke
A field program balances great potential for learning against a major expenditure of resources.

7. Art Galleries and Museums: Nonclassroom Learning for the Nontraditional Student   69
Ruth Schwartz
In the increasingly open market for continuing education courses in art, detailed planning is required, and efforts must be made to meet the expectations of adult learners for personal growth.

8. Learning Through Student Activities 77
Susan A. Morrell, Richard C. Morrell
To optimize the learning potential in student activities, ongoing leadership training and some forms of student activities transcripts or portfolios are necessary.

9. Nonclassroom Learning: A Review of the Literature 89
Jo Ann Carr
The literature provides information on the benefits, implementation, costs, and means of assessing nonclassroom learning. A key factor in implementation is academic leadership.

Index 97

Editor's Notes

Nonclassroom learning is hardly a new phenomenon in higher education. Some aspects of it have been around so long that we have accumulated a significant body of knowledge on them, as in the case of television-based learning, in which a sustained successful track record and an increasing inventory of quality programming exist. The American Association for Higher Education has made available a directory and guide to over sixty programs designed to serve off-campus learners (Lewis, 1983). The directory fosters an appreciation for the potential value of a wide array of telecommunications efforts sponsored by a variety of institutions and cooperative groups. Other areas such as learning in the library are only beginning to receive serious attention by academic administrators. The bottom line, however, shows little overall progress in the integration of nonclassroom learning on most campuses since the publication of *Organizing Nontraditional Study* (Baskin, 1974).

Wartgow, in Chapter One, points to institutional climate as one of the primary reasons for the failure of most institutions to make significant use of nonclassroom learning, and several of the other chapters agree. This position is also underscored by Newman in *Higher Education and the American Resurgence* (1985), in which he presents the strongly held belief of academe that "the role of the faculty is to teach and that the lecture is the appropriate mode for doing so" (p. 64). He further suggests that more active participation in the learning process is threatening to the faculty. If in the past it has not been the inferiority of nonclassroom learning but rather resistance to change on the part of campus personnel, and particularly campus leadership, that has hindered the integration of such learning experiences into curriculums, is there any reason to look for a noticeable increase in the adoption of nonclassroom learning in the next decade? The answer seems to be yes, because the pressures for change are external and growing. They cluster around changing demographics, resource limitations, and national and state pressures for greater quality in education.

With fewer traditional students available for freshman classes, institutions are paying more attention to other sources of students: older students, including senior citizens and women wishing to enter the job market after raising families; minorities; international students; and those located in remote rural areas. This competition for students places increased pressure on institutions both to be attractive to potential students and to explore avenues that can enhance their ability to succeed. If managed well and integrated into the academic life of an institution, nonclassroom learning can receive high marks in promoting both recruitment and retention.

While it has been a generally accepted fact for well over a decade that people learn at different paces and that they have different learning styles, in a seller's market there has been little incentive to provide alternative learning processes. Students of all ages are increasingly sophisticated consumers of all forms of technology, from television to personal computers. To limit their education to classroom lectures is roughly equivalent to restricting movie-goers to old black-and-white silent films. Television in particular is changing learning capacities, and modern technology with its compact discs and VCRs is increasingly raising expectations for learning when and where students find it convenient (especially considering the work and family demands of most nontraditional students). Today, in a buyer's market, there is every reason to develop and promote instruction through alternative delivery systems both to attract students into academic programs and to increase their retention rates. Moreover, the financial constraints caused by decreasing federal dollars and dropping enrollments are strong incentives to explore delivery alternatives that can reach distant learners who would not be served otherwise and that would prove more cost effective than traditional courses.

In response to national studies on the lack of quality in education, educators have called for, and many institutions and states have undertaken, a process of self-examination to improve learning outcomes. Newman, for example, calls for moving beyond passive learning based on the lecture approach to education for creativity, risk taking, and civic involvement. A good case can be made within his argument for a careful examination of nonclassroom learning; indeed, he states: "There is also no reason for the classroom to be the only focus of education. More imaginative use of the library, laboratories, and other learning opportunities can contribute greatly" (1985, p. 64).

Others such as Cross, who is quoted in Chapter Five of this volume, argue further that such learning is also superior because it fosters the mastery of skills that will prepare people for lifelong learning utilizing the myriad informal opportunities available as near as the public library. Indeed, it is perhaps the least documented avenue of nonclassroom learning, learning in the library, that most directly addresses concerns for active learning. Students whose education revolves around resources that will continue to be available to them after graduation gain information-handling skills across discipline borders that allow them to locate and evaluate new information as needed throughout their lifetimes.

One of the sometimes stated and often implied themes in this volume is that, just as the lecture is not the ultimate method of instruction, no other one instructional method is a sufficient addition to an academic institution's instructional repertoire. Stowers and Tessmer, in Chapter

Two, and Purdy, in Chapter Three, make it clear that a wide range of learning resources may be employed in any one course, much less in an entire curriculum. The process for determining which learning approach to use should be built into the curriculum development process of the individual program, and the selection should always be made on the basis of which method will best meet a particular learning need. The major problem in this process is ensuring that the faculty and staff making these decisions will have sufficient familiarity with the options to make good decisions; in Chapter Two Stowers and Tessmer deal with this issue in the most detail. Each of the chapters in some way calls attention to the need to integrate such decision making and such course offerings into the academic mainstream of the campus.

Cost issues as related to institutions and learners are also addressed in each of the chapters. I want to underscore Wartgow's admonition in Chapter One that the establishment of policies and priorities should come before considering budgeting issues. While initial investments in some areas can be substantial, Carr, in Chapter Nine, cites expectations that nonclassroom teaching utilizing technology is expected to net savings in instructional costs over a period of time. Failure to consider the impact of ongoing costs and services on academic and student support services can jeopardize the success of programs, as can insufficient provision of faculty reward systems.

Chapters Three and Four are devoted to television-related learning. It is in this area of nonclassroom learning that long operational program track records can be seen and the best documentation has been done on learning outcomes. (A good body of knowledge is also coming into existence on the learning outcomes of student activities.) Purdy and Wartgow point out the major problem in comparing such approaches with more traditional instruction: Traditional classroom-centered programs have seldom been subjected to rigorous evaluation for effectiveness. Moreover, there appears to be general consensus within this volume as well as in the literature reviewed by Carr that nonclassroom learning, with its emphasis on the individual, requires individualized processes of evaluation. Nonetheless, research generally indicates positive results for nonclassroom learning and in some cases documents higher student achievement through nontraditional approaches (see the studies cited in Chapters Two and Three). Nonclassroom learning in many cases has been documented as having a positive effect on student retention. Beyond the learning outcomes of students, Wartgow adds other evaluative criteria for nonclassroom learning that are of concern to administrators: accessibility, flexibility, personalization, synthesis to learners' goals and other institutional programs, and efficacy of resources. A number of the chapters in this volume underscore the value of nonclassroom learning in meeting the needs of students who would not likely be reached by traditional on-campus courses.

That not all nonclassroom learning is technologically dependent is made clear in chapters Six, Seven, and Eight. Chapter Eight has primary relevance for campuses with major concerns for traditional students; Chapter Seven underscores the value of understanding the needs, interests, and limitations of nontraditional students and constructing the learning situation accordingly. Field experiences, whether a part of students' academic programs or through some types of student activities, can build good ties between learners and their future work environments as well as providing an opportunity to master interpersonal and organizational skills important to future success. The unifying thread that runs through all nonclassroom learning options is, as cited in Chapter Nine by Carr, "an attitude that puts the students first and the institution second, concentrates more on the former's need than the latter's convenience [and] encourages diversity of individual opportunity" (Commission on Nontraditional Study, 1973).

Unfortunately, current value standards and reward systems on most campuses are not conducive to the support of nonclassroom learning. At most universities research scholars, in a league with university presidents and successful football coaches, are considered the stars. Second place goes to classroom lecturers, and third place goes to the wide variety of personnel who serve as the instructional backbone for nonclassroom learning, such as faculty members who oversee field experiences, media designers, librarians, and student affairs personnel. As long as reward systems cannot equitably accommodate a greater diversity of educational contributions, it is unlikely that the institutional climate will ever afford nonclassroom learning anything more than a poor second place, with the result that few learning options will exist for students.

Two chapters in this volume, the first and final chapters, should be considered a must for any administrator seriously contemplating initiating or further expanding one of the nonclassroom learning opportunities discussed in this volume. In the first chapter Wartgow makes a strong case for the candid evaluation of how nonclassroom learning relates to institutional climate. Such a climate, when coupled with the symbolism associated with nonclassroom learning, is likely to mean the success or failure of a program before the first student registers. These issues should be of paramount concern to campus leaders considering the introduction or expansion of nonclassroom learning opportunities as well as to those concerned with institutional changes in other areas. The literature review in the last chapter was conducted within the range of topics to be covered in the volume but independent of their actual writing; therefore, the great majority of the sources reviewed complement rather than duplicate other chapter references. Although more generic in its approach and organized by management concerns such as costs and evaluation, it is not difficult to identify references relating to particular methods of nonclassroom learning.

Another theme documented in the literature search, and which occurs throughout this volume, is the crucial role of academic leadership in the evolving of an institutional climate so that nonclassroom learning can be successfully integrated into academic programming. Nonclassroom learning first received prominent attention in response to the student unrest of the 1960s but by-and-large did not influence the instructional mainstream. The combination of factors, which has again created a students' market, presents a second opportunity for such an enrichment of the academic process. With the availability of better technology and, even more important, a national concern for improved quality in learning outcomes, it is to be hoped that the academic leaders of this decade will accomplish the integration of nonclassroom learning that was only contemplated in the 1960s. This volume of *New Directions for Higher Education* is dedicated to that leadership.

Patricia Senn Breivik
Editor

References

Baskin, S. (ed.). *Organizing Nontraditional Study.* New Directions for Institutional Research, no. 4. San Francisco: Jossey-Bass, 1974.
Commission on Nontraditional Study. "Recommendations of the Commission." *Chronicle of Higher Education,* 1973, 7 (18), 6.
Lewis, R. J. *Meeting Learners' Needs Through Telecommunications: A Directory and Guide to Programs.* Washington, D.C.: American Association for Higher Education, 1983. (ED 227 731)
Newman, F. *Higher Education and the American Resurgence.* Princeton, N.J.: The Carnegie Foundation for the Advancement of Teaching, 1985.

Patricia Senn Breivik is director of the Auraria Library, which serves over thirty-two thousand students and faculty of the Community College of Denver, the Metropolitan State College, and the University of Colorado at Denver. She was a 1983-1984 American Council on Education Fellow in Academic Administration and since then has been serving part-time as special assistant to the president of the University of Colorado.

Differing symbolism and institutional cultures can be major hindrances to the implementation of nonclassroom learning.

Implementing Nonclassroom Learning: Management Considerations

Jerome F. Wartgow

The French poet Paul Valery is credited with the following quotation: "The trouble with our times is that the future is not what it used to be." Nowhere does this statement ring truer than in the minds of seasoned college and university administrators. And while there may be disagreements over the direction and nature of the future, there is little disagreement over the fact that American higher education has entered an era of significant change. The Carnegie Council (1980, p. ii) reflected conventional wisdom when it summarized the consensus as follows: "After thirty years of general and sustained growth, American higher education is entering a period in which each of its three thousand institutions faces a separate and less certain future. Population shifts are altering the demography of the country, budgets are suffering from inflation and restrictions on government spending, the student body is changing and because these factors affect different institutions differently, it is imperative for the leadership team of each institution to make its own projections."

This dramatically changing environment, coupled with rapidly advancing technology, has increased pressure on college and university administrators, structures, and processes to adapt to a new set of conditions. Among the most exciting and frequently suggested strategies for addressing issues of the changing environment are those that involve nonclassroom learning. As a result, higher education managers are likely to find themselves increasingly involved with issues and opportunities of learning that occur outside of the traditional classroom setting.

The concept of nonclassroom learning is not new to higher education managers. The educational literature of a decade ago was replete with admonitions that higher education should experiment with all manner of nontraditional study as a response to pressures of student unrest. There was sufficient interest to warrant publication of a New Directions sourcebook, *Organizing Nontraditional Study* (Baskin, 1974). The observations in it remain relevant today and provide a helpful perspective for considering issues of nonclassroom learning in 1986.

The intervening decade was also a period of heavy activity in nonclassroom learning. New and innovative colleges and universities were established, and existing institutions raced to be more responsive, innovative, and nontraditional than their sister institutions. Today, most, if not all, of our colleges and universities are involved in some activities that fall within the broad definition of nonclassroom learning. Nonetheless, and in spite of an enormous investment of time and energy by dedicated and talented people, nonclassroom learning does not yet enjoy continued and widespread support as a fully accepted and integrated part of academic programming.

The focus of this chapter is on those basic issues that must be addressed if nonclassroom learning is to have a broader and more enduring impact than it has had in the past. The point of view I present is that of a manager who has been directly involved, in several settings, with both successful and unsuccessful attempts to implement nonclassroom learning. Analysis of the reasons for the success or failure of these activities revealed that there were strong influencing factors that received little managerial attention. Traditionally, managers have focused on the collection and analysis of facts related to costs, pricing, and credit-hour equivalencies of nonclassroom learning. Much of this time might have been better spent in analyzing the symbolism and perceptions of various decisions related to nonclassroom learning and in assessing the relative compatibility of the particular activity with the "culture" of the institution. Although these concepts are relatively ambiguous, their influence on implementation of nonclassroom learning is substantial.

Symbolic Considerations of Nonclassroom Learning

Some authorities argue that in complex organizations, such as colleges and universities, symbolism and the subjective perception of an occurrence may be more important than the objective occurrence (Bolman and Deal, 1984). Following this line of thought, facts and rationality may be less important than symbolism and perceptions to managers who attempt to gain support and commitment for nonclassroom learning. There is much symbolism involved in policy decisions related to nonclassroom learning. Unfortunately, each decision symbolizes different things to different people and each symbol has the potential of generating significant political repercussions. These political repercussions, in turn, often influence subsequent decisions and the very nature of the learning activity itself. It is important, therefore, for the manager to analyze the symbolic consequences of each policy that will be made in conjunction with development of the strategy for implementing nonclassroom learning.

The importance of perception and symbolism is illustrated by the variety of interpretations that might be given to answers to the fundamental question: What is the primary purpose of implementing nonclassroom learning? There is, of course, a wide range of possible responses to this question, and it is incumbent on the manager to require program initiators to provide evidence supporting their response before proceeding. However, administrators who have had experience in these matters will be quick to point out that controversies and problems surrounding complex issues such as nonclassroom learning are seldom explained or resolved through logic or rationality. That is why it is important to also deliberately consider the symbolic consequences of accepting a particular statement of purpose. To illustrate, let us consider the potential symbolic perceptions of various responses to the basic question of purpose. Assume first that everyone agrees that the purpose of implementing nonclassroom learning is to institute program revitalization through the injection of innovative instructional approaches. To one constituent group (perhaps students), this statement might be perceived as a positive symbol of a progressive, innovative administration with an agenda for change. To another constituent group (perhaps academic administrators), this same statement might symbolize a direct challenge to the strength of the existing program and the effectiveness of its leadership.

Assume now that the agreed on purpose of nonclassroom learning is to affect economies and efficiencies in the delivery of instruction. This statement might have strong positive symbolism to a board of trustees that is seeking administrative efficiency or to student constituents who relate efficiency to lower tuition and fees. It may simultaneously have negative symbolism to faculty members who envision increased standardization of course work, lower budgets, and potential threats to job security.

Perceptions also extend far beyond the campus. To illustrate, let us this time assume that the agreed response to the purpose statement is to attract new student clientele. This statement might well symbolize very positive things for the faculty, and perhaps the entire university community, who believe that increased resources, job security, and status will accompany new students. At the same time, the statement may be perceived as a negative symbol by another group (perhaps state legislators) who interpret it to be an attempt by the institution to garner more public funds through the accumulation of "cheap full-time equivalents (FTE)." In other contexts, this same statement of purpose could have positive symbolism for certain segments of the community who see the proposal as directly responsive to their desire to gain access to educational programs that were not previously available. However, if for example the institution is a public university, the symbol could be very negative to a community college that perceives that the university wishes to encroach on its special role and service area.

In scenarios such as these, the persons involved in drafting and advocating the purpose statement would likely have never considered the potential for such disparate interpretations of the same statement. Rather, they would probably have been narrowly and inwardly focused on what they considered a rational approach to developing a response to the basic question of purpose. Through a systematic analysis of the potential interpretations of each policy decision surrounding nonclassroom learning, the manager will reduce the ambiguity surrounding the issue and thereby improve the likelihood of successful implementation.

Compatibility with Organizational Culture

A second important managerial consideration relates to the extent to which nonclassroom learning is compatible with the institution's "organizational culture." Organizational culture as used here is not an esoteric concept. It refers to the basic attitudes, characteristics, and personality of the institution. Said another way, organizational culture is "the way things are done around here."

The importance of understanding organizational culture is receiving considerable attention in management and organization literature. Several recent publications (Schein, 1985, Bolman and Deal, 1984, Deal and Kennedy, 1982) suggest that too little attention has been devoted to the manner in which an organization's culture affects how its members think and behave. It is asserted that by understanding organizational culture better, we will be better equipped to understand why some activities fail and others succeed.

Successful implementation of nonclassroom learning will require support, commitment, and compatibility with the values of a large and diverse number of constituents. These constituents, individually and collectively, comprise the culture of the institution. Because each institution, like the people in it, has a unique culture, what will be warmly embraced and successfully implemented on one campus will be flatly rejected and reluctantly paid lip service to on another. Therefore, it is important for the manager to take the time to determine whether or not the proposal fits the culture of his or her unique institution. If it is concluded that institutional climate and readiness is compatible with nonclassroom learning, the manager will be in a position to lend full support and encouragement. If it is found that there is a basic incompatibility between the institution's culture and nonclassroom learning, it will be necessary to consider the consequences of alternative courses of action.

One alternative is to withdraw support for the proposed activity and redirect the associated energy, time, and priority to other projects. This option merits serious consideration if the assessment reveals a strong institutional culture and shared set of values that run counter to those imbedded in nonclassroom learning. A second alternative is to modify the nonclassroom learning activity or the culture or both so as to create a better fit. This approach is worthy of consideration in situations where the assessment reveals a weak institutional culture and relatively little agreement among constituents on basic values. This circumstance provides both an excuse and an opportunity for leadership. Schein (1985, p. 2) has found that organizational cultures are created by leaders, and he concludes that there is a possibility that the "only thing of real importance that leaders do is to create and manage culture." If this assertion holds, then the introduction of nonclassroom learning into a weak-cultured institution may present an opportunity for the manager to rally constituents in the development of shared values, institutional identity, and new enthusiasm for academic program development.

Administrative Considerations

When full managerial consideration has been given to the issues of symbolism and organizational culture, the manager and the institution will be ready to tackle the detailed issues of implementation. The literature on theories and tools that can be utilized by managers in the planning and implementation of nonclassroom learning activities is extensive and readily available to interested readers. Therefore, no attempt is made here to provide models of methodological approaches to planned change. There are, however, several issues that have not received attention commensurate with their importance to successful implementation of nonclassroom learning. These are briefly summarized in the next sections as a reminder to managers that consideration of each at the outset will help avoid difficult issues later on.

Definition of Nonclassroom Learning. It is important that nonclassroom learning be clearly defined for management purposes. This should not be an exercise in semantics that is oriented toward communication with external constituents. Rather, it should be viewed as necessary to clarify internal relationships so that ambiguity can be reduced and appropriate structures for implementation can be established.

The first task of definition involves the establishment of criteria for determining which specific programs, activities, and classes are to be conducted in a nonclassroom setting. It is not the purpose of this task to attempt to identify specific programs that will emphasize nonclassroom learning. Rather, the intended outcome should be a framework for evaluating the circumstances and conditions under which nonclassroom learning will take place. These determinations have important implications for subsequent activities such as the development of pricing strategies, establishment of productivity relationships between faculty members in classroom settings and those in nonclassroom settings, and the adoption of evaluation procedures. This process will also provide an opportunity to resolve, prior to implementation, sensitive in-house political concerns over perceived competition for students and resources between the "new" programs and the institution's traditional classroom-centered programs. Finally, early identification of the criteria under which nonclassroom learning will take place will also serve the purpose of responding to anticipated questions of program quality.

A second task of definition centers on the clarification of issues related to assignment of responsibility for nonclassroom learning within the institution's organizational structure. Failure to deal with organizational relationships at the outset contributes to confusion later on. In addition to obvious administrative advantages, clear establishment of responsibilities within the institution has powerful symbolic value. It signifies to both internal and external constituencies the relative priority and level of importance assigned to nonclassroom learning.

Professional and Legal Issues. There is a morass of professional and legal issues surrounding nonclassroom learning. Federal, state, and local governments, accrediting associations, and a myriad of coordinating and regulatory agencies all have an interest in nonclassroom learning. If the activity involves the use of telecommunications or other forms of high technology (which most do), the legal entanglement with external organizations is even greater. Therefore, it is important to obtain competent legal advice early in the process. Heeding the advice of a knowledgeable attorney can prevent unnecessary false starts, embarrassing future litigation, and undue delays in implementation. Involving attorneys, however, is not without its risks. Without specific delineation of responsibility and close supervision, attorneys all too often behave in a manner that John Naisbitt has likened to beavers—that is, they jump in the mainstream and dam things up. Managers will need to be firm and persistent in clarifying for their attorneys the distinction between executing policies and killing programs.

Budgetary Issues. Techniques and strategies for funding and pricing nonclassroom learning activities have received much attention. Nonetheless, it is the budgetary issues that often present the major obstacle to implementation. Unfortunately, these budgetary obstacles often arise long before issues of compatibility with institutional culture and problems of program definition have been resolved. Most managers feel more comfortable addressing the knowns of budgeting than the unknowns of nonclassroom learning. As a result, they often become prematurely immersed in a quagmire of technical minutiae and quantitative detail. This diverts them from the more important task of establishing policies and priorities. While managers cannot and should not avoid the question of how much a program will cost, they must be careful to maintain a perspective that views nonclassroom learning within the larger context of academic program development. Once the priority for nonclassroom learning has been decided, the resolution of budgetary issues will occur in the prior context. Too often, the process is reversed and the answer to the cost question determines the institutional priority.

Evaluation. The fundamental evaluative question is: Do the differences make a difference? Notwithstanding the fact that traditional classroom-centered programs are rarely subjected to rigorous evaluation for effectiveness, the burden of proof is on advocates of nonclassroom learning to demonstrate that the educational benefits of the particular experience justify doing things differently. Traditional evaluative efforts and models are seldom satisfactory for the task of evaluating nontraditional programs. Therefore, it will be necessary to devise new models of evaluation that relate specifically to the unique structure, form, and clientele of nonclassroom learning. My associates and I have suggested elsewhere that any such model should attempt to assess impact in five general categories: accessibility, flexibility, personalization, synthesis, and efficacy of resources (Wartgow and others, 1974).

The accessibility component of the evaluation model should be an examination and analysis of the extent to which the nonclassroom learning experience is serving the needs of the particular segment of the population for which it was designed. The pertinent questions are: Is access to education provided for a population who normally or formerly did not attend college or who were not satisfied in previous educational experiences? Are those who are usually considered educationally disenfranchised (minorities, low income, the elderly, and those with diversified work and life patterns) taking advantage of the nonclassroom experience?

The evaluation model should also consider the extent to which nonclassroom learning provides flexible alternatives to general patterns of instruction. Questions that must be addressed are: Does the new experience provide flexibility in terms of time, content, and process? Are entrance requirements and admissions procedures designed to be flexible? Is flexibility provided for designing unique programs related to the individual's educational goals? Are the learning modes flexible?

The new student clientele and changing environmental conditions suggest that our colleges and universities must be more responsive to individual needs. Therefore, a personalization component of the evaluation model should seek answers to questions such as the following: Are the nonclassroom learning experiences individually satisfying? Do support services provide for personal interaction? Is there evidence of self-determination of programs to meet individual goals?

Another important component of the evaluation model is that which attempts to determine how well the nonclassroom activity is synthesized with the learner's educational background and goals and with other institutional programs. Answers to questions such as the following may be useful in making this determination: Is the nonclassroom activity an integral part of a larger institutional educational program? Does the learning activity facilitate a synthesis of related educational and life experiences with the individual's goals? Does the experience help the student to acquire knowledge or skills necessary to succeed in life? What has the student really learned from the nonclassroom learning experience?

Finally, one component of the evaluation model for nonclassroom learning must provide information on the extent to which the activity represents an efficient use of resources. Managers must be prepared to search for answers to the following: Is this an effective use of resources within the context of accomplishing the institution's goals? Does this activity provide the same (or better) quality education for less money? less time?

Development of an evaluation model for nonclassroom learning as a precondition to implementation will contribute to refinement of the statement of purpose and to the resolution of many of the other issues previously discussed. But perhaps most importantly, it will also symbolize the commitment of the institution to the pursuit of quality in its nonclassroom learning endeavors.

Conclusion

Nonclassroom learning activities provide a tremendous opportunity for many colleges and universities to adapt efficiently to the rapidly changing higher education environment. It is important, however, that there be a fit between these new activities and the basic attitudes, characteristics, beliefs, and culture of the institution. Higher education managers are encouraged to deliberately and systematically assess this level of compatibility as part of the process of deciding whether or not to proceed with implementation. Attention to these items and the related administrative considerations of program definition, budgetary, legal, and professional issues, and evaluation models will enhance the potential of nonclassroom learning as a significant influence on the future direction of higher education.

References

Baskin, S. (ed.). *Organizing Nontraditional Study.* New Directions for Institutional Research, no. 4. San Francisco: Jossey-Bass, 1974.
Bolman, L. G., and Deal, T. E. *Modern Approaches to Understanding and Managing Organizations.* San Francisco: Jossey-Bass, 1984.
Carnegie Council on Policy Studies in Higher Education. *Three Thousand Futures: The Next Twenty Years for Higher Education.* San Francisco: Jossey-Bass, 1980.
Deal, T. E., and Kennedy, A. *Corporate Cultures.* Menlo Park, Calif.: Addison-Wesley, 1982.
Schein, E. H. *Organizational Culture and Leadership: A Dynamic View.* San Francisco: Jossey-Bass, 1985.
Wartgow, J., Curtis, D. V., and Laird, D. "Evaluating Nontraditional Studies: Implications for Public Policy." In R. Cope (ed.), *Public Policy: Issues and Analyses.* Tallahassee, Fla.: Associatoin for Institutional Research, 1974.

Jerome F. Wartgow is executive director of the Auraria Higher Education Center in Denver. He has also held positions as deputy executive director of the Colorado Commission on Higher Education and as director of research and evaluation at Governor's State University, where his responsibilities included development of the assessment model for the university's nontraditional programs.

Self-paced instruction can offer flexibility to students and academic institutions alike, but careful planning is required.

Self-Paced Instruction

Michael P. Stowers, Martin Tessmer

Self-paced instruction is an instructional method that continues to grow in use through all levels of American education. It can be used to satisfy the learning needs of a wide variety of traditional and nontraditional learners and to address institutional problems such as distant learners, low-enrollment courses, student recruiting, and faculty overload. For these reasons, administrators who have not seen this method widely implemented on their campuses should give it serious consideration. The purpose of this chapter is to outline the issues and procedures relevant to the successful implementation of self-paced instruction in higher education.

Background

Self-paced instruction is an arrangement in which individual students set their own schedule for learning and monitor their own progress (Good, 1973). Most important, students are allowed to progress at their own rates through some unit of instruction.

Various forms of self-paced instruction have been used sporadically in American classrooms since the mid 1800s (Kulik, 1982), but only recently has it come to the forefront of education. Since the 1960s, self-paced learning has reemerged as an influential instructional force primarily because of four developments. First, the development of programmed instructional materials in the 1960s stressed self-paced instruction and self-instruction.

Second, individualized systems of instruction were developed and widely implemented at all levels of education (Gagne and Briggs, 1979). Systems such as Individually Prescribed Instruction (IPI) and the Personalized System of Instruction (PSI) utilize self-paced methods. Third, the development of Computer-Assisted Instruction (CAI) has made self-pacing more prevalent, since most CAI allows students to progress at their own pace. Finally, the proliferation of instructional videotapes, auditory materials, and other media has freed more course time from a group-paced format.

While self-paced learning is but one feature of an instructional program, it is often used to designate an entire approach to learning. Actually, self-paced learning may include other features such as mastery learning, frequent testing with immediate feedback, lecturing, and proctoring. This means that various forms of self-paced learning may differ from one another in important instructional aspects. Self-paced instruction has been successfully used in a variety of subjects and in a variety of formats. It has been successfully used in courses on botany, speech communication, reading, educational psychology, and esthetics (Kapfer and Kapfer, 1972). In particular, many self-paced programs have been developed in the sciences. Self-paced instruction has been used to teach factual information, concepts, principles, problem solving, and psychomotor skills (Gagne and Briggs, 1979). A variety of learning materials may be used, including audiotapes, videotapes, computer programs, print study guides, and self-instructional texts.

Advantages of Self-Paced Instruction

Student Advantages. The major intended advantage of self-paced instruction is to allow students to learn at a rate compatible with their abilities. Educators such as Carroll (1963) and Bloom (1968) believe that learners of different aptitude or ability levels can master the same learning outcomes when each is allowed sufficient time. Differences in aptitude reflect differences in learning time requirements, not in the ability to learn.

Frequently, self-paced instruction takes the form of a series of small units (modules), each of which is a complete lesson in itself (Kemp, 1985; Keller, 1968). These self-contained modules allow students to skip over lessons that they already know and select what they want to study next— an attractive feature to students. In addition, self-paced instruction allows flexibility for scheduling learning time, which is useful to students who have heavy workloads or family obligations. Moreover, the location for learning can be quite flexible, allowing students to study at home or in convenient off-campus locations.

In reviewing the effectiveness of several widely used self-paced instructional programs (Keller's PSI and Postlethwait's A–T), researchers found student achievement to be generally higher in self-paced courses than in more traditional courses (Kulik and others, 1979; Kulik, 1982). Particularly in postsecondary education, student achievement in and attitudes toward self-paced instruction have been favorable. There is also evidence that self-paced students become better managers of their learning, which can transfer to other courses (Wang and Walberg, 1983).

Instructor Advantages. For instructors, the advantage of self-paced instruction is that they can be freed of instructional responsibilities that they may find repetitious and boring. In self-paced instruction, the instructional materials may assume the primary role of delivering instruction (Keller, 1974). The instructor can then choose to work individually with students (Kemp, 1985), host group discussions to clarify misunderstandings, or to present the social-political implications of course topics (Keller, 1968). The role of the instructor changes; the instructor becomes more the manager of instruction and less the vehicle for transmission of information.

Institutional Advantages. A number of benefits can accrue to the institution that uses self-paced instructions. With a reasonably extensive use of self-paced courses, an institution can offer a wider variety of classes and subjects in any one semester than would otherwise be possible. For required courses with traditionally low enrollments, the institution can avoid the problem of needing to direct students into underenrolled classes or operating them at a loss. Also, since the instructor serves as a manager and not a group lecturer, the instructor is free to "teach" more courses at a given time.

For courses in which faculty expertise is not particularly strong, self-paced instruction can utilize purchased or produced materials to upgrade the quality of the courses. For courses in which faculty expertise is strong, having the faculty organize the course and produce or choose the instructional materials can ensure high instructional quality of the course in the absence of those faculty members. It also means the course can be made available at remote sites or other campuses within a multi-campus system. In either scenario, periodic updating and revision of the self-paced course can maintain the quality of the course across changes in time and teachers.

Self-paced instruction can also be used to increase enrollments and recruit students. Self-paced courses allow variable entry and exit times for courses, so that students do not have to follow the semester "clock" to register and complete their coursework, which can enhance recruitment efforts with a number of target markets. The portability of these self-contained modules means that self-paced courses can be offered in a variety of locations convenient to potential students. Such programs can also be offered to talented high school students. The students earn college credit, and the college has a good opportunity to attract these high-caliber students to their campus. Self-paced learning can also relieve the stress placed on academic resources such as libraries and laboratories. The students' variable rate of lesson completion will spread out the demand for specific resources, which avoids the problem of having all the students wanting the same resources at the same time.

Disadvantages of Self-Paced Instruction

There are some potentially serious disadvantages to self-paced instructional programs. Most, however, can be eliminated or minimized through proper planning.

Student Disadvantages. One recurrent disadvantage is student procrastination. When left to schedule their own learning, some students will procrastinate until the end of the semester or course deadline. This tends to place a heavy workload on instructors and their assistants toward the end of the course schedule, reducing the efficiency of the instructional program. Such students are more likely to withdraw from the course or to do poorly on final examinations (Santogrossi and Roberts, 1978; Glick and Semb, 1978). This disadvantage can be minimized by giving students unit-completion calendars and by periodically monitoring students' progress. Also, some instructors use a modified self-paced schedule in which all students must reach a certain unit by a given date or suffer a grade-point penalty (Reiser, 1984).

Another potential disadvantage is the lack of student-teacher interaction when the self-paced course materials are the *sole* source of instruction. Without some opportunities to meet with instructors, students may feel either abandoned or that the course is not a "real" course. Therefore, the instructors should plan period instructor-learner activities such as small group discussions or individual meetings and be readily available to students through well-publicized office hours and telephone communications. For remote-site learners, arrangements must also be made for access to an instructor or assistant.

Instructor Disadvantages. While an instructor's teaching time may decrease in a self-paced course, the time needed for organization and preparation of the course can increase dramatically. In general, the more "teacherless" and self-directed a self-paced course program becomes, the more structure, organization, and clarity must be built into the instructional materials, orientation information, and tests. Instructors have to compose study guides, write more tests, and adapt or produce instructional media. If instructors are not given the proper lead time and administrative support, they can quickly become disenchanted with the self-paced process. The problem can be obviated by granting the following: lead time and release time for course construction, credit for retention or promotion, and support personnel such as teaching assistants and secretarial support. Most importantly, the instructor should be involved in the initial planning process for the course. These issues are further discussed later in this chapter.

Institutional Disadvantages. In many self-paced programs, the learner can enter and leave the course-offerings systems at a variety of times. This flexibility adds dramatically to the administrative functions of the institution. The admissions, registration, and business offices must understand and support the flexibility that such instruction is designed to offer and establish procedures to support such flexibility. In an open entry and exit program, students must be free to register, pay, and complete a course with a grade in less or more time than a normal semester or quarter. Such requirements are likely to require a change in institutional functions such as record-keeping. In cases in which such administrative adjustments cannot be made, self-paced courses have been successfully used on a semester or quarter schedule although they lose some of their attraction for nontraditional students.

Fostering Self-Paced Instruction Within the Institution

Organizing a Task Force. To foster self-paced instruction on campus, it is essential that there be an administrative commitment to making these opportunities available to students. This commitment includes fostering a climate in which faculty and staff understand why the institution is committed to self-paced instruction and what steps are involved in developing and maintaining an effective program. Because self-paced instruction can affect every facet of the campus organization, a good way to create the desired climate is to establish a task force that includes a cross-section of the affected departments. This task force should include the teaching faculty, the support staffs of central service groups, a media designer, and others with experience in developing self-paced instruction.

Through workshops, demonstrations, and site visits, the task force can be educated in the workings of self-paced learning. Potential projects can be discussed and plans made to identify programs that could be enhanced through self-paced instruction. For example, although self-paced courses have been taught in every discipline, subject areas that have lent themselves best to self-paced learning are the sciences and computers. The task force should be maintained after the program has begun and should be continuously informed of its progress.

After a reasonable period of implementation, the task force should evaluate the program, according to its utility to both the institution and the student. The information gained from the evaluation should be used to either eliminate the program or strengthen it through revision. One of the most important evaluation criteria must be the evaluation of learning outcomes achieved through self-paced methods as compared to traditional group-paced methods. If the former is not as good as the latter, and if ways cannot be determined to improve the self-paced course, it should be eliminated. This same thorough evaluation should be used for off-campus or on-campus programs, for in-house or purchased self-paced courses. In all cases, the results of the evaluation should be widely disseminated on-campus.

Involving Academic Units. Once the institutional base is established, the decision to pursue a self-paced option becomes the final decision of the normal planning process within academic units. Once a new course is agreed on, the unit should discuss the pros and cons of traditional versus self-paced options. The choice of instructional method will depend on a variety of factors developed in the normal support assessment, such as: (1) development time available, (2) faculty willingness, (3) teaching assistance granted, and (4) production and service support. If the institution has a variety of support services in television, art, photography, and media design, the decision may well be to adopt self-paced instruction and produce the materials on-campus. However, the unit should understand that a wide variety of materials are available from off-campus suppliers. Entire courses can be bought or rented, allowing a department to offer a self-paced course that could not be offered any other way, owing to a lack of on-campus talent or departmental overload.

Organizing Course Development Teams. After the self-paced course projects have been agreed on, working teams should be established for each course project, and a team leader should be identified. The leader is usually the faculty member managing the course or the media designer. The team's first charge should be to develop a budget and time frame for project completion. The completion activities should include developing orientation, instruction, and testing materials and methods, as well as plans for project evaluation and revision. The team should report periodically to the academic unit or task force to ensure progress.

Faculty and Staff Involvement

Faculty Involvement. One of the first steps in project planning is to identify instructors who are willing, able, and available to develop and administer self-paced courses. Suggestions for faculty members can be obtained from campus media designers, learning-center staff, continuing education personnel, and academic unit directors. If the same faculty members are suggested by different sources, they are likely candidates.

In general, instructors involved in this type of work require a high degree of drive and commitment to self-paced learning. They need to understand the learning process and be willing to adapt and modify their subject to the requirements of the selected technology. Because technology plays such an important part in the support of self-paced learning, the instructors must feel comfortable with the technology and understand how it works. The ability to organize, plan, visualize, and communicate verbally is essential. Faculty members who develop and offer the course must see themselves as managers or facilitators of learning (Keller, 1968, 1974). They continue to be the persons who most influence the content of the course, but they require the help of a variety of support staff to build, teach, and evaluate the course.

Support Personnel Involvement. The type of support personnel required to create an on-campus program of self-paced instruction will vary, depending on the length, complexity, and size of the course. Usually the staff includes clerical and media design personnel. Graphics, photography, television, and computer support help may also be required. If not available on campus, campus vendors' staff members are available but expensive.

Continuing Involvement. Once the course preparation is completed and the course ready to be offered, there must be a continuing commitment of faculty and staff time to its operation and improvement. The creators and implementors of the project should expect several cycles of evaluation and revision even with purchased, prepackaged courses. Both in-house and purchased courses require knowledgeable people to maintain personal contact with students and staff and to coordinate the course. Course planners must ascertain that the flexible scheduling afforded self-paced learners is reflected in the hours and assistance of course-related student services. For example, the course materials must be available at a variety of times and may have to be distributed at various locales. Similarly, instructors or course assistants must be available at a range of times, whether that availability means in person, by phone, or by computer link. Self-paced courses attract a wide variety of nontraditional students, such as older, handicapped, distant, or English-as-a-second-language learners. In every case, the services available to students must be clearly articulated to them at the outset of the course and regularly updated. Newsletters, notices, and electronic bulletin boards have all been successfully used for updating.

Administrative Concerns

Course Credibility. In offering self-paced courses, there should be no differentiation between traditional and self-paced courses for purposes of credit, grading, testing, and record-keeping. Such differentiation could allow for "second class" degrees. Self-paced courses should also be listed alongside regular courses in the catalogue. It helps, however, to promote them so that the benefits and freedoms of self-pacing are clearly understood.

Course Orientation. Since some students have difficulty in assuming responsibility for their own learning, orientation sessions are vital. These sessions can be on- or off-campus and can allow the instructor to provide information, distribute course materials, and set deadlines. Additional course meeting times may be offered on an individual or group basis, to keep the work flow steady and the learner motivated. If distance education is part of the program, scheduled teleconference sessions can be used.

Course Ownership. When courses are developed in-house, there must be a written agreement between the faculty and the administration about course ownership. A common policy is that the faculty member is paid for the course development directly or through release time (Keller, 1968; Lewis, 1971). Therefore, no additional compensation need be offered through the life of the course, unless substantial updating or revision is required. In any case, ownership agreements should conform to institutional policy and be processed in a similar manner across different self-paced projects.

Promotion and Tenure. A central issue is the promotion and tenure credit a faculty member can receive for developing or implementing a self-paced course. Such credit can be a strong motivation for faculty interested in self-paced instruction. Moreover, the level credit assigned is also a measure of the institution's endorsement of the program. For personnel decision making, development or implementation work can be considered part of normal teaching activities, with release time and teaching credit being granted. However, if such assignments are given to instructors in addition to regular teaching loads, they can be evaluated as overload assignments, with due credit given.

Costs

The cost of self-paced instruction is not necessarily less than that of traditional teaching. In particular, the advance costs may be higher than starting a new course in the traditional manner. This includes costs of preparing and duplicating new materials and training instructors and staff in conducting self-paced instruction. However, with repeated use of an established self-paced course, costs fall appreciably (Kemp, 1985).

The cost structure varies with the instructional methods and materials used and is influenced dramatically by the location of the student. If distance education is involved, the cost of campus-student communications and student services can be a high-ticket item. The form of the communication may vary, but most likely it will include mail and telephone communications, which are expensive. The costs of these services may be recovered through increased student fees; or if courses are offered on-site for industry or business groups, the company may well pay the additional costs in return for employee convenience. Such costs must be clear to all parties before the course begins.

Finally, course costs also rise when large amounts of equipment or materials are involved or when there are large student enrollments, and additional fees may be assessed to defray these costs. Since class sizes can vary from three to four hundred students per course, faculty teaching loads can escalate to half- or three-quarter-time for one course. However, if the course load is properly assigned, the funds received through extra enrollment can compensate for faculty work load costs.

Summary

Self-paced instruction has a history of application and success and is applicable to a wide variety of disciplines and learners. While it is an effective instructional method, the advantages and disadvantages of self-paced instruction should be carefully considered before making a commitment to its implementation. Once an institution incorporates self-paced instruction into its institutional mission, planning and development groups must be organized from diverse institutional elements. These groups can help identify viable courses and instructors, ensure that adequate support is available to the faculty, and ensure that support systems are responsive to student needs.

The real winner in these development efforts will be the learners. For some, self-paced instruction represents a course designed to suit their abilities and life situations. For others, it represents their only chance to enroll in a course. Through these student benefits, the institutional benefit will be increased enrollments.

References

Bloom, B. S. "Mastery Learning." *Evaluation Comment*, 1968, *1* (2).
Carroll, J. "A Model of School Learning." *Teachers College Record*, 1963, *64* (8), 723-733.
Gagne, R., and Briggs, L. *Principles of Instructional Design.* (2nd ed.) New York: Holt, Rinehart & Winston, 1979.
Glick, D. M., and Semb, G. "Instructor-Set Pacing Contingencies Versus the Absence of Such Contingencies in a Personalized University Course." *Journal of Personalized Instruction*, 1978, *3* (3), 131-138.
Good, C. V. *Dictionary of Education.* (3rd ed.) New York: McGraw-Hill, 1973.
Kapfer, P. G., and Kapfer, M. B. *Learning Packages in American Education.* Englewood Cliffs, N.J.: Educational Technology Publications, 1972.
Keller, F. "Goodbye Teacher." *Journal of Applied Behavior Analysis*, 1968, *1* (1), 78-89.
Keller, F. "The Basic System." In F. Keller and J. Sherman (eds.), *The Keller Plan Handbook.* Menlo Park, Calif.: W. A. Benjamin, 1974.
Kemp, J. *The Instructional Design Process.* New York: Harper & Row, 1985.
Kulik, J. A. "Individualized Systems of Instruction." In H. E. Mitzel (ed.), *Encyclopedia of Educational Research.* (5th ed.) New York: Macmillan, 1982.
Kulik, J. A., Kulik, C. C., and Cohen, P. A. "A Meta-Analysis of Outcome Studies of Keller's Personalized System of Instruction." *American Psychologist*, 1979, *34* (4), 307-318.
Lewis, J. L. *Administering the Individualized Instruction Program.* West Nyack, N.Y.: Parker Publications, 1971.

Reiser, R. "Reducing Student Procrastination in a Personalized System of Instruction Course." *Educational Communication and Technology Journal,* 1984, *32* (1), 41-49.

Santogrossi, D. A., and Roberts, M. C. "Student Variables Related to Rates of Pacing in Self-Paced Instruction." *Teaching of Psychology,* 1978, *5* (1), 30-33.

Wang, M. C., and Walberg, H. "Adaptive Instruction and Classroom Time." *American Educational Research Journal,* 1983, *20* (4), 601-626.

Michael P. Stowers is director of audiovisual services and associate professor of education technology at the University of Nevada, Las Vegas.

Martin Tessmer is assistant professor of instructional design, Media and Telecommunications division, Auraria Library, Denver.

Telecourses, which can offer quality learning experiences, can be an effective means of serving nontraditional students.

Telecourses: More Than Meets the Eye

Leslie N. Purdy

A review of reports concerning the use of television and telecourses by higher education institutions throughout the United States and Canada reveals a significant growth, both in the number of institutions utilizing this medium and in the number of students learning by television. After years of false starts, experiments, research, and innovations that often were not incorporated into the mainstream of instructional offerings, use of television for instruction is becoming institutionalized. Colleges now offer telecourses semester after semester, and the number of telecourses available makes it possible to offer a telecourse curriculum that has diversity and depth. Institutions have developed procedures for acquiring, broadcasting, and teaching telecourses as well as for serving the needs of telecourse students. Use of telecourses has to be considered an example of the successful use of technology in instruction.

Since schools began considering television's educational potential, the record has alternated between experimentation and rejection. Precise and reliable figures about the use of telecourses have been difficult to ascertain. There were no national or state-by-state reports of student enrollments, college adoptions, or broadcast arrangements. In 1978-79, two national surveys were done that provided the first hard data regarding television use nationally. The first of these surveyed two- and four-year institutions, and its findings included these startling statistics: 71 percent of the 2,993 institutions surveyed made some use of television; 61 percent used television for instruction. Seven hundred thirty-five colleges offered a total of 6,884 courses on television in 1978-79, an average of nine courses per college. Those colleges enrolled 498,000 students in the television courses, an average of seventy-five per course (Dirr and others, 1981). Four-year institutions were more likely to use television in the classroom or on campuses, whereas two-year institutions allocated proportionately more of their effort to off-campus instructional uses. The second national survey focused on television usage at two-year colleges and found that 349 two-year colleges reported offering approximately 2,300 courses on television in 1978-79, generating approximately 162,000 enrollments (Dirr and others, 1980). Indications are that these figures have increased since the surveys were conducted.

One of the most popular telecourses has been "Understanding Human Behavior," an introduction to psychology course, which by spring 1985 had enrolled over fifty thousand students nationwide since its release in 1981. An unknown number of general viewers, over and above those taking the course for credit, have watched and learned from the programs. Another popular course, "The New Literacy," an introduction to computers, produced by the Southern California Consortium for Community College Television, has enrolled over thirty-five thousand students from the time of its release in spring 1984 through fall 1985.

All this suggests educational institutions are willing to commit considerable resources and energy to the use of television for instruction and specifically to the use of telecourses. The record also reflects a great deal of activity by educational organizations, television producers and broadcasters, and foundations in the production and distribution of instructional television in the last fifteen years. Two of the most significant steps are the creation of a national educational television network by the Public Broadcasting Service (PBS) in 1982, the PBS Adult Learning Service (ALS), which now offers telecourses to schools nationwide, broadcast over PBS stations; and the grant of $150 million by The Annenberg School of Communications in 1981 to the Corporation for Public Broadcasting to create innovative and high-quality college-level television materials.

No higher education institution can decide *not* to use educational television because of a lack of information or assistance about the practical aspects of the undertaking. Reports, articles, case studies, and guidebooks are now available that provide this kind of information for educators. Some of the most useful references are: Froke and others, 1981; Perry, 1977; Purdy, 1983; Schramm, 1977; Zigerell, 1986; and Zuber-Skerritt, 1984.

The most important question that educators must address before making a decision to offer telecourses is: Why should we become involved in the use of this new technology? An institutional decision to offer telecourses can eventually become a major commitment of institutional personnel, time, and money, especially if the decision includes producing and broadcasting television programs. Because the medium of television is new to most administrators and faculty, the decision must also include a commitment to education and a period of time for trial and error. The decision to use television cannot be made casually or lightly, or the result will be unsuccessful for everyone involved, including the students. Consequently, before making the decision, administrators and faculty need to understand why instructional television is important and what it can and cannot do for the institution.

Television as a Major Medium of Communication and Expression in Western Culture

Whether or not it is true that in the United States today there are more television sets per capita than bathtubs, the fact is that television is an incredibly popular and powerful medium. Television is replacing the printed word as the most influential mass medium and, as such, has been blamed for many things, from newspaper failures to the decline in the reading level of college students. Children watch an average of twenty-seven hours of television per week, and adults watch about thirty-five hours weekly. Researchers study the effects on viewers of the quantity and subject matter of the programs, and commentators and analysts of our culture are probably correct in likening the impact of this new technology with the invention of the printing press.

These concerns about the nature and impact of television are often shared by faculty and administrators who maintain that we need to promote *more* reading, *more* writing, and *more* lecturing in teaching to counterbalance television's impact. But there are two problems with this position: First, it ignores the fact that there is no turning back the clock; that television, for good or ill, is here and will continue to increase its role in society. For higher education not to deal with this new medium is to risk creating a serious gap in communication between a print-oriented faculty and students who have grown up watching television. Second, although television may be different from the written word in how it conveys knowledge, it is not inherently better or worse than the written word. Common sense tells us that knowledge can be conveyed through all forms of communication.

Therefore, the question for higher education institutions should not be whether or not to be involved in television. To ignore television is to separate the institutions from modern culture and to prevent exploration of the advantages of the medium for instruction. The challenge becomes determining how television should be used for learning and what the institution's role should be in the creation and dissemination of instructional television. And in reply to the suggestion that using television to teach will reduce student's abilities to think, write, and speak, it must be noted that telecourses available today require students to read texts, interact with the faculty (often in written communication as well as face-to-face), write, study, review, and do exercises and projects, as well as watch television programs. Telecourses do not rely on television alone to convey the content of a course, but rather are carefully designed to use several media, ideally exploiting the particular strengths of each.

Television as a Way to Reach New and Traditional Students

Research has documented that the profile of students attracted to telecourses does differ from that of the campus students. Whether called "distance learners," "adult learners," or "lifelong learners," students attracted to telecourses tend to be older, busy with a job or homemaking responsibilities, and attracted to the convenience of studying at home and maintaining part-time enrollment. In terms of the students' socioeconomic characteristics, they have many similarities to younger students enrolled on campuses.

Telecourses have not proven to be particularly effective in reaching so-called disadvantaged students, those who because of race, income, or prior education find attending traditional higher education institutions difficult. And yet, the profile of telecourse students does suggest that telecourse instruction can make higher education institutions more accessible by attracting students who cannot or will not come onto campus for classes. And as new telecourses are created, the subjects covered and support systems devised should be intended to reach more students for whom higher education presents barriers.

Information about the students enrolled in telecourses has been detailed by two recent research projects. The first was conducted by Instructional Telecommunications Consortium members in 1984, with data collected from forty-two two-year colleges offering telecourses (Brey and Grigsby, 1984); the second was a study of students enrolld in Annenberg/CPB telecourses in the fall of 1984 in both two- and four-year institutions ("Research on Student Use of the Annenberg/CPB Telecourses in the Fall of 1984," 1985). Among the findings were the following:

1. Over two thirds of the students were female, although the percentage varied from state to state and from course to course.

2. Only 23 percent of the students were of traditional college age, eighteen to twenty-two years old. Almost half of the students were thirty or older.

3. Approximately two thirds of the students were married or divorced. Over half had at least one dependent.

4. About 80 percent were employed, over half employed full-time.

5. About 20 percent were enrolled only in the television course and were new students drawn to the college by the television course. 40 percent were enrolled for ten or more credit hours, and for two thirds of the students, this was their first television course.

6. Eight out of every ten students intended to view the television programs at home. This was especially true for students who were older, female, married, and not concurrently enrolled in on-campus courses.

7. The educational backgrounds of telecourse students varied widely, both in type of course and type of institution offering the course. Overall, 20 percent were enrolled in their first semester of college, while another 20 percent had already earned at least an associate degree, even though most of the sample came from two-year institutions.

8. In the Annenberg/CPB sample, almost half of the students indicated that they hoped to achieve a master's or doctoral degree. More than a third hoped to complete a bachelor's degree.

9. Over half the students enrolled in the telecourse because an on-campus section of the course would conflict with their work or leisure time.

There were major differences in the characteristics of students according to the subject matter of the telecourse. Data-processing telecourses, for example, attracted older students who wished to do their coursework off-campus. A greater number of these students had already completed a higher education degree and could be categorized as students using the telecourse as a refresher course or to gain knowledge in an area not studied in previous college courses. Students enrolled in more traditional general education telecourses were more likely taking the course to fulfill degree requirements.

The profile of telecourse students revealed in these studies shows some similarities to that of a group in our society described as the "new-collar class," ("The New-Collar Class," 1985). These people tend to be employed in service industries, pursue education periodically to improve their employment level or to change occupations, place a high value on education and see it as important for gaining economic and occupational security, and tend to pursue educational opportunities for self-enrichment. Some telecourse students may be drop-in students who sample educational opportunities from a variety of educational institutions. Others appear to take telecourses as a way of testing their ability to do college-level work and, if successful, go on to enroll in other courses (both telecourses and campus-based courses) at the institution, with the goal of completing a degree. The new-collar class is a large and growing population that will continue to seek out educational opportunities that are conveniently tailored to their needs and schedules.

In summary, telecourses can be offered by higher education institutions as a way of attracting students having any of the following motives:

those wanting to eventually complete formal degree requirements, those returning after interrupted education, employed people seeking continuing education for job upgrading or changing occupations, those seeking self-enrichment opportunities, older students who are frightened at the idea of competing with younger students in a classroom setting, and women who have young children at home but have difficulty obtaining and affording acceptable child care.

Finally, telecourses are not only a form of distance education but should also be seen as a viable way to offer students quality instruction on campuses. Whether offered as television-based courses over closed-circuit television or as videocassette independent study courses, telecourses can be offered on-campus. The University of Southern California School of Business Administration offers its graduate students both video- and audio-based instructional packages as part of its graduate degree program. Stanford University and Pennsylvania State University offer telecourses to their undergraduate students. Technologies such as Instructional Television Fixed Service (ITFS), cable television, videocassettes, and videodiscs will only expand the ways television can be used as part of a college's total instructional program.

The Growing Number of High-Quality Telecourses

A look at catalogues of telecourses currently available reveals that most of the quality telecourses have been produced in the last five years (for example, the *Catalog of Mass Media Courses*, 1985). Before that, unless colleges made a commitment to produce programs locally, there was little to choose from. And while those experimental schools that did local production made important strides, they did not create telecourses that were designed for widespread adoption.

One development that first demonstrated the educational power of television was the "wraparound" course produced around major PBS series. In 1975 *The Ascent of Man* attracted a record number of viewers, and a record number of students enrolled in a course offered in conjunction with the series, produced by the Extension Division of the University of California–San Diego and Miami-Dade Community College. Such courses permitted colleges to experiment with offering telecourses without much financial risk, since air time on PBS stations was underwritten by sponsors. Criticisms of wraparounds included the following: They did not fit existing discipline classifications; faculty members had little opportunity to prepare to teach the course for the first airing, and second and third airings were not always broadcast at convenient times, if offered at all; and in some cases wraparounds represented one point of view and therefore were questioned as being appropriate for credit courses. As a result, colleges could rarely incorporate wraparound courses into their regular catalogue of course offerings; neither could institutions count on having more than two broadcasting per year.

However, whatever the weaknesses of the wraparounds, they demonstrated two important facts: There were students out there who would enroll in a broadcast telecourse, and colleges could take advantage of broadcast television, whether through cooperation with PBS stations, cable casting, or commercial stations.

In the 1960s several institutions began producing telecourses that were visually exciting and designed as college-level courses, usually involving local academic advisers and national advisory committees and consultants. General education courses such as introductory biology, American history, introductory psychology, marriage and the family, and many "how-to" courses were produced, mainly by two-year colleges such as the Coast Community College District (California), Dallas County Community College District, and the Southern California Consortium (a group of thirty-five two-year colleges). In order to recover the money invested in production, these producing institutions marketed and distributed the courses on a lease basis, with the lessee having the responsibility of securing local broadcast time.

These early telecourses established models that have become common at the undergraduate level: twenty to thirty half-hour television programs; printed materials consisting of a text or book of readings and a carefully prepared study guide; and local implementation of the course, determination of course classification, specific requirements, and credit granted. National or regional "open universities" have been proposed to offer telecourses but, for the most part, telecourses, while not produced locally, become local course offerings. Maintenance of local control is probably an important reason faculty members have overcome their resistance to using acquired course materials when offering telecourses.

Additional improvement in the inventory of available telecourses is attributable to the Public Broadcast Service's Adult Learning Service. Serving as a distributor for telecourses produced by a variety of institutions, it lists courses in the fine arts and humanities, social sciences, international studies, business and technology, and teacher education. The ALS listing is now also being enriched by courses resulting from the Annenberg/CPB Project. This is a fifteen-year project funded by Walter Annenberg to support higher education for adults through telecommunications. Major PBS series and telecourses such as *Brain, Mind, and Behavior, Congress: We the People,* and *The Mechanical Universe,* a two-semester physics course, have been produced through the Annenberg/CPB Project. These new courses are often appropriate for upper division and even graduate or professional level credit. However, the pattern of individual institutional adoption and implementation has continued (*Fact Sheet, Fall 1986,* 1985).

Although the number of telecourses available has been increasing rapidly, some topic areas are still not represented; these include vocational-technical courses, physical and natural sciences both for the major and the nonmajor, and business courses. As schools increase their television options, they will be able to target courses for specialized audiences such as continuing education for nurses, teachers, unions, and government workers. The number of educational and commercial producers will grow, permitting users more choices and control over local telecourse offerings.

Telecourses as Effective Instruction

Perhaps the most important question that can be asked about telecourses is: How well do they teach? No instructor or administrator wants to offer an instructional system that fails to deliver. As a new and often experimental approach, television has been studied regularly since the 1950s. When television instruction has been compared to traditional teaching methods—used to teach a wide variety of subjects, in many different settings—no significant difference has been found. In fact, in several studies television has been found to be a superior form of instruction.

In what is now considered a classic study, research was conducted on the telecourses offered by Chicago T.V. College in the late 1950s. The college offered an A.A. degree through broadcast telecourses, thus making the findings especially significant for similar programs today. Research techniques were careful, objective, and validated. The summary finding stated that "when evaluated by the techniques of measurement and analysis used in the experiment, television instruction is a thoroughly effective means of extending college opportunities to at-home students in all the subject areas explored in the experiment" (Zigerell and Chausow, 1974, p. 34).

In an attempt to allay criticisms of telecourses, many colleges have undertaken local research projects. None of the findings conflict with experimental research, and most have reported student enthusiasm for telecourses. These studies rely on measures of the gains of students in mastering objective course contents. For some instructors, the findings conflict with their personal conviction that students learn more, and learn more of significance, through face-to-face interaction with instructors and other students. The problem is that it has not been possible to evaluate clearly these more subjective, complex, and elusive kinds of learning, either for classroom instruction or for telecourses. Thus, for some faculty members, skepticism will remain their response to all the research findings about telecourses.

All the research studies have helped to document that student success in telecourses is related primarily to three factors: their motivation, age, and previous educational backgrounds. More mature students who have the motivation and learning skills necessary for independent study have a greater likelihood of success in telecourses than students lacking these characteristics. These findings have implications for administrators and faculty members using telecourses. Telecourse promotional materials should stress for discipline and study skills required for those taking telecourses. Schools must provide testing and feedback to students early in the course to quickly identify students with difficulties and to provide assistance. Distance-learning situations make such identification and assistance more difficult. In short, telecourses are not for everyone and will not take the place of good classroom-based instruction for students who want and need that learning environment.

Conclusion

Despite the expanding use of telecourses, some administrators and faculty members will continue to be skeptical about the potential for using television for instruction. For some, the often unspoken fear is that using television for instruction will result in a loss of jobs for teachers. For others, just the difficulty of learning new teaching techniques and adjusting to new patterns of student interaction are difficult obstacles to overcome. The whole institutional environment is an important factor: No matter how enthusiastic an individual teacher may be about using television, unless colleagues and administrators support and encourage such efforts, the individual is unlikely to persist in experimentation.

The current problems of maintaining and expanding enrollment in colleges nationwide may, in the end, be the main reason many schools will turn to telecourses. With the decline in the pool of the traditional eighteen- to twenty-four-year-old college students, many institutions are adopting programs and delivery systems that appeal to and reach part-time students, older students, and distance learners. Television offers a way of reaching these students and, thus, of increasing enrollments. The availability of new and effective telecourses makes it possible to use television for this purpose.

References

Brey, R., and Grigsby, C. *Telecourse Student Survey, 1984.* Austin, Texas: The Instructional Telecommunications Consortium and the American Association of Community and Junior Colleges, 1984.
Catalog of Mass Media Courses. Washington, D.C.: American Association of Community and Junior Colleges, 1985.
Dirr, P. J., Katz, J. H., and Pedone, R. J. *Higher Education Utilization Study, Phase I: Final Report.* Washington, D.C.: Corporation for Public Broadcasting, 1981.
Dirr, P. J., Kressel, M., and Pedone, R. J. *Instructional Uses of Television by Two-Year Colleges, 1978-79.* Washington, D.C.: American Association of Community and Junior Colleges, 1980.
Fact Sheet, Fall 1986. Washington, D.C.: PBS Adult Learning Service, 1985.

Froke, M., Radzyminski, W., and Spring, M. (eds.). *Telecommunications and Higher Education.* Pittsburgh, Pa.: Institute for Higher Education, 1981.

Perry, W. *The Open University: History and Evaluation of a Dynamic Innovation in Higher Education.* San Francisco: Jossey-Bass, 1977.

Purdy, L. (ed.). *Reaching New Students Through New Technologies.* Dubuque, Iowa: Kendall-Hunt, 1983.

"Research on Student Use of the Annenberg/CPB Telecourses in the Fall of 1984." Washington, D.C.: The Annenberg/CPB Project, February 1985.

Schramm, W. *Big Media, Little Media.* Beverly Hills, Calif.: Sage Publications, 1977.

"The New-Collar Class." *U.S. News and World Report,* September 16, 1985, pp. 59–63.

Zigerell, J. J. *A Guide to Telecourses and Their Uses.* Costa Mesa, Calif.: Coast Community College District, 1986.

Zigerell, J. J., and Chausow, H. M. *Chicago's T.V. College, A Fifth Report.* City Colleges of Chicago, January 1974.

Zuber-Skerritt, O. *Video in Higher Education.* London: Kogan Page, 1984.

Leslie N. Purdy is director of Alternative Learning Systems at Coastline Community College, Costa Mesa, California.

Opportunities are expanding for on-site instruction to the business and industry communities.

Interactive Television

Michael Bisesi, B. Dell Felder

More money is spent today by American corporations on employee development than is spent to operate all public higher education institutions. The information age intensifies the need for lifelong education. The professional life spans of most fields are becoming shorter and shorter, and increasing numbers of working adults need opportunities to update their knowledge and skills.

The needs of high-technology industries have spurred many universities to develop interactive instructional television programming. In the state of Arizona, for example, it is estimated that high-technology companies in Phoenix alone will require almost fifteen hundred new engineers each year, a need that greatly exceeds the state's educational capability (Greenberg, 1985, p. 3). Arizona State University developed its Interactive Instructional Television Program (IITP) in the early 1980s as part of a multi-million-dollar engineering excellence program. Like many systems of its kind offered by an increasing number of universities around the country, ASU's IITP provides convenient and cost-effective educational opportunities for employees of high-technology firms.

The Need for Interactive Television

In the late 1960s, the School of Engineering at the University of Southern California (USC) became interested in using telecommunications technology to take courses off-campus to employees of local industry. A large number of part-time students who worked in high-technology firms were taking courses leading to a master's degree. Often they would commute long distances, usually at night, to attend class, and rarely were they able to take more than one course per semester. Because it took so long for students to complete the program, material they learned was often obsolete before their degree had been earned. The industry needed a more efficient method to deliver advanced degrees and continuing education to engineering students who could not conveniently attend classes on-campus.

The University of Southern California decided to develop a television system capable of broadcasting "live" courses to students in remote sites. At that time, two other university-based television systems existed. One was in Florida, where large numbers of engineers who worked at Cape Canaveral were receiving graduate instruction through television from the University of Florida at Gainesville. In Texas, the Tager System linked together several educational institutions and industrial organizations.

At about this same time, Stanford University began to design an area-coverage network to reach the heavy concentration of high-technology companies in the San Francisco bay area. Both the Stanford and the USC networks use the Instructional Television Fixed Service (ITFS) band of frequencies set aside by the Federal Communications Commission (FCC) in the early 1960s for educational use (Munushian, 1985, p. 40). Until this time, these frequencies had been used solely by public school systems for instructional broadcast on a non-interactive basis. About the time universities became interested in use of these frequencies, the FCC in 1968 permitted use of a portion of the ITFS band for playback using FM radio.

Recently the exclusive use of these channels by educational institutions has been in jeopardy. Because the channels were not being fully utilized, in 1982 reallocation of some of the twenty-eight channels for other than ITFS use was proposed. The threat that channels might be allocated to commercial entities for multiple distribution service (MDS) spurred action by many educational groups to obtain licenses and retain exclusivity of use. While the controversy is not yet settled, it is likely that the FCC will seek a resolution that will not endanger the operation of ITFS programs by educational institutions. It is possible, however, that ITFS and MDS operators may eventually share this channel space.

Instructional Television Fixed Service Operation

Today, many universities, including the University of Florida, Georgia Institute of Technology, the University of Illinois, Iowa State University, the University of Minnesota, Oklahoma State University, and the University of Washington, offer credit courses and continuing education through ITFS. Most university ITFS programs originate in campus classrooms and are sent to remote sites. For example, at Arizona State University, ITFS programs originate in four studio-classrooms located on campus. A television signal is carried from these classrooms by an underground fiber optic link across campus to a television studio where it is beamed to a transmitter located outside the city. Because the ITFS signal is of low power, a second transmitter is needed to receive, strengthen, and rebroadcast the signal to other locations in the Phoenix area. Remote sites are equipped with special dish antennas and converters to receive the ITFS signal and to modify it for VHF reception on standard television sets.

On-campus students enrolled in ITFS courses attend class in the studio-classrooms, which contain loudspeaker-telephones to facilitate interaction with students at remote sites during the broadcasts. These classrooms are equipped both with broadcast-quality color television cameras for reception of live instruction and with color monitors for student viewing. An IITP video technician operates the cameras, which function by remote controls from an adjacent control room. The cameras track the instructor's movements, and they transmit the image from a letter-sized pad located on the instructor's desk, which instructors use much as they would a chalkboard to illustrate concepts or transmit written information. Slides, films, and videotapes are also used in presentations.

Students off-campus view the classes at various specially equipped receiving sites and are able to interact with the instructor and with other students via telephone. Desk-mounted microphones broadcast the questions and comments of students in the studio-classroom to remote sites. Students at remote sites may dial into the studio-classroom to ask questions or participate in discussions. A low-level buzzer and light indicate to the instructor that a caller is waiting. Both the student's questions and the instructor's response can be heard by all students in the studio-classroom and at remote sites that often provide features such as speed dialing and a conference phone set to make it easier for students to contact the instructor (Greenberg, 1985).

A courier service delivers and picks up materials daily from each remote site. Tests, homework, handouts, and other types of instructional materials are distributed and returned in this way. A coordinator located at each site handles the logistics of managing the program at the site.

Academic Quality Assurance

The administrative decision to implement an ITFS program should go beyond mere questions of a technology-oriented curriculum to examine larger campuswide concerns. The most important issue facing administrators considering the use of interactive television is the question of instructional quality. If academic quality cannot be maintained, or if the mission of the institution might be compromised, then use of interactive television must be seriously questioned. To begin, interactive television should not be considered in isolation. Often, institutions treat their various academic components, from general education and graduate studies to self-paced instruction and interactive television, as separate agenda items for institutional planning purposes. Chickering (1969, p. 196) disagrees with that approach, arguing that "curriculum arrangements, teaching patterns, and evaluation procedures are systematically linked." Considering these elements separately is unwise, since "to modify one part without threatening the others is impossible" (p. 69).

The decision to use interactive television should be considered within the total curricular and instructional context of the institution. Any assessment of interactive television requires some determination and assessment of the benefits of the expected outcomes of that instruction. Administrators should thus attempt to assess interactive television within this design framework by attempting to determine if such an approach enhances or inhibits the development of desired student competences and experiences. It could certainly be argued, in the context of research by Cross (1976), that interactive television takes us beyond education for all and toward education for each. There could clearly be new opportunities for focusing on individualized instruction, mastery of learning, self-paced modules (by using videotapes of previous courses), cognitive styles, personal development, and interpersonal skills.

But why is the institution doing this? Will its academic standing be improved? Will its students learn more? Will its students have access to needed resources, such as library and computer services? Will its students be able to interact with other students and faculty in a productive manner? Bisesi (1984) provides a general framework of program evaluation that could include interactive television. The institution should assure itself that degree or other program objectives presented by the academic departments can actually be met through ITFS instruction. Faculty qualifications, adequacy of support facilities, and student satisfaction are additional areas of concern.

A growing number of institutions are reporting successful ITFS programs. The Continuing Professional Development Division of the American Society for Engineering Education (ASEE) provides a forum for dissemination of information about ITFS. Growing out of interest that developed during the 1984 College Industry Education Conference, ASEE published the *1985 Compendium of Uses of Instructional Television in Engineering Education in the United States*. This compendium describes ITFS programs that operate in more than twenty-five American universities. Some of these programs have operated successfully for more than two decades (Chenette and Biedinbach, 1985).

In summary, decisions about the use of interactive television, rather than being made by individual departments, should be made in consideration of overall curricular and instructional strategies of the institution. Most importantly, decision makers should not permit interactive television to be simply an expensive electronic correspondence school.

Justifications for Interactive Television Use

If quality can be maintained, the question of "fit" with the institution's needs in the delivery of its educational services must be addressed. For example, if the need is to reach underserved populations, then the justification for using interactive television may be fairly clear. However, the need is less clear if the motivation is simply to boost sagging enrollments. Peterson (1979, p. 61) rightly contends that televised instruction may be the only means of reaching some groups of students such as geographically isolated persons. The need to reach such student populations has been reported by many institutions using IITP as a primary reason for establishing the program. Julian (1982), however, did not find any demographic difference between students who enroll in televised courses and those who take on-campus courses. The only rationale for such course enrollments seemed to focus on convenience, interest in the content of the courses, and an opportunity to earn credit.

Since interactive television requires specifically prepared receiving sites, it is not clear whether ITFS courses may one day be a means of serving large untapped student populations in private homes. Except for cable systems in Columbus, Ohio, and The Woodlands, Texas, very few homes are wired for interactive television. Should channels one day be shared by ITFS and MDS operators, however, broadcasting into private homes would become feasible. The broadcast could be sent from a university ITFS to a commercial cable company, which in turn could broadcast via cable into private homes. Homeowners could interact with the university instructor by telephone. Should this technology become widespread in American homes, new educational outreach ventures could become attractive possibilities for many universities.

Justification of Cost

Like all new technologies, interactive television is expensive. Factors that should be considered in resource allocation decisions are of particular concern. Griffin and Burks (1976, pp. 63-64) provide a general model for appraising administrative operations, which includes unit objectives, parameters, unit operations, personnel, finance, facilities, unit organization, and tools and processes used to coordinate action. Lapin indicated in an earlier study (1963) that televised instruction requires a reasonable cost per student, a large number of students, multiple channels for different programs, and local control. More recently, Froke (1981) offered three models that illustrate how televised instruction might fit administratively, either as an instructional service, a "miscellaneous" model that is essentially laissez-faire entrepreneurship, or an open learning model that focuses on individualized instruction.

Providing instruction through ITFS does pose cost considerations not typical of on-campus instruction. Remote sites require management. Materials must be distributed and collected from students, tests must be proctored, lessons may need to be videotaped for later use, and technical difficulties may require attention. Sites should be staffed with personnel competent to facilitate the program. Site coordinators are often employed by companies cooperating with the university in the ITFS program. If this is not the case, the university may need to assume the costs of providing site management personnel. There are also instructional costs associated with developing and teaching ITFS courses. Professors may need release time to prepare courses for television. The cost of instructional materials such as slides, overhead transparencies, models, student handouts, and the like must be considered. Travel to and from remote sites by couriers, site coordinators, or others may be involved.

Most universities have developed a pricing structure that combines student tuition with a fee from participating companies. Companies are normally expected to pay costs of equipping the sites with receiving and playback equipment. In addition, they are often charged a fee that recovers capital costs of developing the system. Student tuition is also charged. At Arizona State University, students enrolled in IITP pay regular tuition, and companies with remote receiving sites are charged $80 per credit hour taken by students enrolled at their site. Illinois Institute of Technology charges tuition plus a service charge of 20 percent of the tuition. At Stanford University, participating organizations pay a membership fee as well as student fees. The University of Southern California charges tuition plus a television surcharge of $50 per credit.

Costs for building an ITFS system can be substantial. In a report titled "Update on PBS/NNS Technical Considerations for Station Managers," presented at an annual meeting attended by ITFS managers in May 1985, costs estimated for a ten-watt system were as follows ("The Cost of Being on ITFS System," 1985, p. 27):

Tower	$24,000–$100,000
Transmission	$125,000
Microwave System	$ 98,000
Test Equipment	$ 43,900
Control Room Equipment	$135,000–$195,000

These cost estimates do not include the antennas, down converters, cable, and so on for the reception sites served by the system. Typically, the receiving organizations or institutions purchase their own reception equipment.

Ingredients of Success

Most ITFS proponents indicate that success depends in large measure on following a few simple rules. First among these is recognition that mass media message cannot be "injected" whole into an audience (Schramm, 1971). To be effective, mass media messages must "interact" with an individual's characteristics. It is important, therefore, to understand the composition of the ITFS target audience and to design instruction for that audience.

Most of the students served through ITFS are working adults, and their special characteristics as learners must be considered. They are usually highly motivated, self-directed persons with an accumulated reservoir of experience that can be an important resource in their learning. Their learning orientation is toward accomplishing tasks and solving problems associated with their jobs. They have a high concern for immediacy of application and limited tolerance for subject-centered instruction. They prefer a problem-centered focus, especially if it is illustrative of problems they encounter.

Perrin (1976) suggests that the most effective methods for presenting material via ITFS seem to be instructional television as part of a mixture of relevant learning materials. A number of components are involved, but primary among them is some kind of personal contact. One study revealed that "even the most nominal person-to-person contact is the critical element in the successful utilization of ETV and open broadcast—critical to student involvement, student retention, student perseverance, and student achievement" (Eyster, 1976, p. 110). Because ITFS is capable of providing this crucial personal contact, it would appear to be a most promising instructional delivery system.

Generally, the professor who is effective as a teacher in the normal on-campus classroom will be successful as an ITFS instructor. Effective ITFS teachers are concerned about presenting information in ways that aid their students' understanding of the material. They provide clear examples, use visual aids, and are willing to exchange information and ideas with students. They are considerate of the needs of students at remote sites to ask questions and clarify concepts. They encourage and facilitate interaction between themselves and their students. Effective ITFS instructors structure their courses so that students are informed of the topics to be discussed in advance of class sessions and are aware of course requirements and assignments. While it is important for ITFS instructors to plan and organize class presentations carefully, they should also be capable of maintaining a flexible approach in the classroom. Situations sometimes arise that interfere with the most carefully laid plans.

The effectiveness of remote site personnel is also important to the success of ITFS programs. If the site is located at a participating company, the site coordinator should understand the employee development needs of that company and be able to provide leadership for that effort. Site coordinators should be competent in establishing systems that permit receiving and sending student course materials in a timely fashion and maintaining accurate student records. They should be effective troubleshooters, able to handle technical difficulties with equipment should they arise.

Planning and assessing instruction are important to the success of ITFS. Content experts, media experts, and students should all be part of the planning and assessing process. At Arizona State University, staff members trained in instructional design work with faculty members on a one-to-one basis to assist them in planning and assessing instruction. Remote site coordinators meet monthly with ASU personnel to discuss problems and suggest improvements. A large number of data useful for assessing the effectiveness of ITFS courses have been obtained from personnel involved in the program. Feedback has been solicited from students, faculty, site coordinators, camera operators, and officials of cooperating businesses and industries. Each semester, ITFS courses are evaluated, and information is used for program improvement.

Summary

As technology improves in general, the potential for university use of ITFS as a means of delivering educational service could become even greater. Universities seeking partnerships with business and industry can find ITFS a highly attractive alternative to traditional on-campus instruction. While the cost of these programs can be substantial, the opportunities provided by them may make the expenditure an investment in the future viability of higher education in our rapidly changing, information-oriented society. Successful ITFS programs are operated with understanding and concern for the needs of the students being served. Organization and planning is stressed. Faculty and remote site coordinators are selected for their competence as teachers and facilitators of learning.

References

American Society for Engineering Education. *1985 Compendium of Uses of Instructional Television in Engineering Education in the United States.* Washington, D.C.: American Society for Engineering Education, 1985.

Bisesi, M. "Program Evaluation: A Qualitative Planning Tool." *Planning and Changing,* 1984, *15* (3), 144–151.

Chenette, E. R., and Biedinbach, J. M. (eds.). *Uses of Instructional Television in Engineering Education in the United States.* Washington, D.C.: American Society for Engineering Education, 1985.

Chickering, A. W. *Education and Identity.* San Francisco: Jossey-Bass, 1969.

Cross, K. P. *Accent on Learning: Improving Instruction and Reshaping Curriculum.* San Francisco: Jossey-Bass, 1976.

Eyster, W. "ETV Utilization in Adult Education." *Adult Leadership*, December 1976, p. 10.

Froke, M. "Administration Issues in Telecommunications." *1981 Current Issues in Higher Education*, 1981, (5), 11-14.

Greenberg, S. "Planning Advanced Education Through Advanced Technology: The Interactive Instructional Television Program at ASU." In E. R. Chenette and J. M. Biedinbach (eds.), *Uses of Instructional Television in Engineering Education in the United States.* Washington, D.C.: American Society for Engineering Education, 1985.

Griffin, G., and Burks, D. R. *Appraising Administrative Operations.* Berkeley: University of California Systemwide Administration, 1976.

Julian, A. A. *Utilizing Telecommunications for Nontraditional Instruction in the North Carolina Community College System.* Durham: North Carolina Consortium for Instructional Telecommunications, 1982. (ED 224 957)

Lapin, S. "On-Air, Closed-Circuit Instructional Television: The 2500 Megacycle Band." Paper presented at Conference on Educational Television, New York, August 21, 1963. (ED 002 491)

Munushian, J. "The University of Southern California Instructional Television Network." In E. R. Chenette and J. M. Biedinbach (eds.), *Uses of Instructional Television in Engineering Education in the United States.* Washington, D.C.: American Society for Engineering Education, 1985.

Perrin, G. "Synopsis of Television in Education." *Educational Technology*, 1976, *16* (5), 7-9.

Peterson, R. E., and Associates. *Lifelong Learning in America: An Overview of Current Practices, Available Resources, and Future Prospects.* San Francisco: Jossey-Bass, 1979.

Schramm, W. "The Nature of Communication Between Humans." In W. Schramm and D. F. Roberts (eds.), *The Process and Effects of Mass Communication.* Urbana: University of Illinois Press, 1971.

"The Cost of Being on ITFS System." *E-ITV*, 1985, *17* (b), 27.

Michael Bisesi is associate dean of the College of Business Administration at the University of Houston-University Park, Texas.

B. Dell Felder is dean of the faculty at Arizona State University West, Phoenix.

Library resources and personnel can be better utilized to promote the institutional learning goals.

Library-Based Learning in an Information Society

Patricia Senn Breivik

The academic library is often the most underutilized instructional resource on campus. Although the concept of nonclassroom learning has appeared in general higher education literature for many years, almost no attention has been paid to learning in the library. Certainly the recent literature on the lack of quality in education has almost entirely ignored libraries. The exception is Newman's (1985) report for the Carnegie Foundation for the Advancement of Teaching. Although it does not address the instructional potential of libraries, it does deal with concerns regarding gaining access to materials within the information explosion.

Rationale for Expanding the Educational Role of the Library

There are several good and immediate reasons for aggressively exploring learning in the library at this time. First, few responses to current concerns for quality in education are "new," and it is questionable whether simply more of the same responses will produce any measurable and lasting improvement. Second, there is general recognition that this and all future generations must exist in an information society. Initial campus responses across the country included requiring computer literacy, which usually meant computer-programming courses. This approach has already been discarded in theory if not in practice, and no alternative approach has been generally articulated. Moreover, information literacy goes beyond computer literacy and "means raising the level of awareness of individuals and enterprises to the knowledge explosion and [to] how machine-aided handling systems can help identify, access, and obtain data, documents, and literature needed for problem solving and decision making" (Horton, 1983, p. 16). Libraries, as the point of access to most information on campuses, certainly deserve close scrutiny for their potential role in educating people for the demand of today's information age. Third, libraries represent a major investment, and it would be administratively short-sighted not to explore contributions—beyond those historically provided by way of resources and services—libraries can make toward meeting an institution's goals and objectives. The biggest hindrance to such an exploration is largely an attitude that perceives libraries as the heart of the institution, which like physical hearts are ignored until a problem arises (for example, negative accreditation reports). This attitude also perceives librarians as passive second-class citizens of academe.

Library-based learning has been slowly evolving in a wide variety of ways on most campuses. Usually labeled library or bibliographic instruction, such efforts have been largely promoted by librarians with little or no administrative support, and they have been largely directed at helping students to perform better in particular courses. The efforts have varied from library orientations to full-credit courses to competency requirements. More recent pressures, prompted by a concern for excellence, have been causing a broader group of academicians to consider information literacy as a necessary component of core curricula or as part of basic skills programs. For example, a 1983 conference entitled "A Colorado Response to the Information Society: The Changing Academic Library" pulled together academic vice-presidents, library directors, and faculty leaders from both public and private institutions. The speakers were academic administrators and faculty members who cited firsthand experiences with using libraries in nontraditional ways and the resultant benefits for learning and research. Subsequently, one of the governing boards made enrichment funds available for a series of follow-up conferences on particular discipline areas and their relation to information and libraries. Miami-Dade Community College has made a major effort to develop and publicize a program called "Information Skills for the Information Age," and Alverno College, which has offered "an ability-based" education since 1973, will be adding an information studies support area to its curriculum in the fall of 1986.

Recognition of the need to prepare students for lifelong learning incorporates the need for students to be able to construct information-search strategies to locate, evaluate, and effectively use information no matter where or how such information is stored. Such an approach is well within keeping with Newman's (1985) concern for active learning that can prepare students for risk taking and citizenship responsibilities. Traditional approaches such as using textbooks, providing reading lists, and putting selected materials on reserve do not, however, provide students with the information-handling skills required for continuing learning after graduation. Neither do these approaches ensure that students will know if they are applying their problem-solving abilities to an appropriate information base. Advocates of nonclassroom learning such as Cross (1979) have for some time promoted the learning potential of libraries: "Although I have been one of the staunchest advocates and promoters of individualized self-paced instruction in the schools, for the ultimate in self-paced instruction, nothing can compete with libraries. . . . Libraries are a unique national resource. They share some learning advantages with television, some with museums, some with schools; they supplement learning in some instances and provide the only opportunity of their kind in other cases" (p. 16).

Developing a Library-Based Learning Program

As campuses continue to seek ways of improving the quality of instruction within resource limitations, the role of library-based learning should be explored within established instructional planning procedures. Whether the administration is identifying minimum competencies or value-added education, or a faculty committee is considering a new core curriculum, or the academic planning is contained within individual schools and tied into program reviews—whatever the planning approach —library-based instruction should be incorporated into the regular planning processes. This is important if the institution is to accept a more visible instructional role for the library and library personnel and if such a role is to be effectively incorporated into the educational goals and objectives of the campus. Administrators can help facilitate such interaction by (1) ensuring that the question is raised as to the educational role of academic libraries or information literacy in an information age, (2) encouraging placement of librarians (and faculty members who have made other than traditional use of libraries in their teaching) on key curriculum planning and evaluation committees, and (3) providing support as needed to allow faculty members to visit campuses or bring in consultants from campuses that have successful library-based learning programs of the type determined appropriate to their own institutions.

Methods of providing library-based instruction vary from lectures to self-paced workbooks to video productions, and easy access to existing models is available through state and national clearinghouses. The selection of methodologies should be based on

- The desired learning outcome, for example, improved performance in a particular class or basic skills development

- Methodologies used in skills areas
- Numbers of students involved
- Availability of resources.

In practice more than one methodology will probably be needed. As more states and higher education institutions are concerned with basic competencies, one approach or set of approaches may be needed to accommodate all beginning-level students and another to provide information-handling skills within students' major areas of study. Several models that have proven successful over a period of time are included in the following list:

1. Since 1977 students at the University of Wisconsin at Parkside have had to meet competency-based requirements in four areas before the junior year, one of which is a requirement in library skills and writing research papers. When students cannot pass the competency test, they may take prescribed courses to meet the requirements.

2. Self-paced workbooks were pioneered at the undergraduate library at the University of California at Los Angeles. Originally developed for educationally disadvantaged students, the program was later expanded to include others. This approach, which has been utilized across the country, is particularly popular when large numbers of students must be reached and when a self-paced option is preferred. Brigham Young University allows students to score their own pretests to determine which areas of the workbook they need to study.

3. Videotapes or slide-and-tape presentations are difficult to produce well but can provide effective learning experiences for both classroom and individual use. The Auraria Library in Denver has produced a series of such tapes, which are usually combined with a question-and-answer period and are scheduled into courses by faculty members in high-need areas such as general research skills (two levels), business resources, and government documents. The Marriott Library at the University of Utah has produced a commercial quality set of very short color videotapes about individual library services. Similar to television commercials, each advertises a single service such as interlibrary loans and stimulates an information awareness that can be a first important step toward information literacy.

Of particular concern in competency approaches is a campus- or system-agreed-on definition of information literacy or of basic information-handling skills. Such definitions are essential to ensure that library-based learning experiences are properly focused and to provide proper evaluation mechanisms. Such definitions will also provide a rational basis for determining how much time is required for mastery. Although definitions will vary at different institutions, a working definition might be:

> Information literacy is the ability to obtain and evaluate information effectively for a given need.

Information literacy is
- An integrated set of skills (research strategy, evaluation) and knowledge (of tools and resources)
- Developed through acquisition of attitudes: persistence in research, attention to detail, and caution in accepting the printed word and single sources of information
- Time and labor intensive
- Need-driven (a problem-solving activity)
- Resistant to changes in resources and technology
- Distinct but relevant to "literacy" and "computer literacy."

Information literacy is not
- (Only) knowledge of resources
- Library dependent (as sole source of information)
- Information finding (it is understanding and evaluating).

Historically, library research skills may have been seen as necessary only for four-year or graduate students, but in our information society basic information skills are needed by all students. Research done at Brooklyn College in the 1970s addressed the particular needs of the academically disadvantaged to learn to cope with information overload and to develop information-management skills (Breivik, 1977). The statistics and responses of those involved in the research experiment all pointed to the fact that "the weekly program of correlated library and information retrieval assistance can contribute to the academic success of disadvantaged college freshman and to student use of the library" (p. 67).

Once into major areas of study, methodologies for library-based instruction have generally fallen into one of several categories: individual professors setting aside a certain amount of time in one or more courses, encouragement of students to take a general research course, or a departmentally required literature-of-the-field course.

Unless departments clearly agree on the amount and level of instruction, the first approach is generally fairly expensive in organizational effort and offers no assurance of a minimum level of learning by all students. The second approach suffers from these same weaknesses as well as not allowing for an in-depth study of the resources of the field and how to evaluate them (whether from on-line data bases, government agencies, or libraries) because of the broader scope of the course. The major concern with the third approach is the addition of another required course to an often heavily prescribed curriculum.

Ideally, an approach different from all of these would be taken; the faculty would consistently construct assignments around information available in or through the library and other community and academic resources. This would mean that in many courses, instead of assigning a textbook, putting materials on reserve, and lecturing, professors would (with the appropriate involvement of a librarian) provide assistance to students in mastering information research strategies and then turn students loose to find their own learning resources. An experiment to foster this type of learning environment was undertaken at Monteith College at Wayne State University beginning in 1960 (Knapp, 1966). The project "called for the establishment of a structure and machinery for a new kind of relationship between librarians and teaching faculty . . . [in which] they attempt to devise course assignments which would involve extensive and meaningful student use of library resources" (pp. 11-12). Although much good information was forthcoming from the project, even in a new college setting it proved largely impossible to change established faculty patterns of teaching. Since Newman's more recent observations (1985) would imply that the faculty response would be similar today, this avenue of providing for library-based learning may represent the ideal, but it does not currently represent a practical alternative to the three previously cited ones.

Faculty and Cost Considerations

Once the learning outcomes are agreed on, the same planning procedures used in any discipline area should be followed to make the decisions regarding the methodologies to be used, the time and credit to be allotted to such efforts, and how the library-based learning experiences will be evaluated. The only difference will be (particularly at the upper division and graduate level) the involvement of both classroom faculty and librarians. The question should also be raised as to who will develop the learning materials and facilitate or teach the library-based learning. If program faculty do not evidence support for the library component and are not involved in its offering, there will be little motivation for students to learn. However, having the library-based learning as part of graduation or competency requirements can at least ensure student participation.

If primary responsibility is assigned to librarians, either additional library staff will need to be hired or other means found to ensure adequate attention to library operations. Questions of faculty status for librarians on some campuses and criteria for retention, promotion, and tenure for librarians on others should eventually be assessed in terms of growing involvement in curriculum planning and instruction. To assign primary responsibility to classroom faculty is to place additional heavy demands on them to keep actively abreast with an ever-increasing information base in a broadening range of types of resources. While this may be a reasonable expectation within a professor's area of specialty, it is much more questionable within the broader discipline area. If such requirements are expected of the classroom faculty, they will need release time from other responsibilities. Whatever the decision, some degree of teamwork will be required. In general, the most promising approach would be thorough advance planning by both classroom faculty members and librarians and shared responsibility for evaluation, leaving the actual program development and delivery to library personnel.

Decisions as to what approach to take in offering library-based learning will dictate the costs involved. Just as in other areas of instruction, costs will be largely personnel-related unless a decision is made to produce self-paced, media, or computer learning packages or programs. When delivery options and alternative staffing arrangements can be identified, cost considerations can be one of the determining factors in the planning of the program. Other equipment needs may also occur, such as a video projector to allow the teaching of on-line data-base searching to classes.

Faculty Development

Discussion of library-based learning would not be complete without some consideration of faculty development. Particularly on campuses whose library and media resources and services are housed together, libraries are natural sites for faculty development activities. In the introduction to papers delivered at the conference "Library Instruction and Faculty Development," the conference host (Suput, 1980) concludes: "The success of both faculty development and library instruction is dependent not only upon greater understanding of the substantive aspects of the two movements, but also upon two other efforts: a spirit of cooperation, and attitudinal change (p. vii)."

There is a tendency for campus concerns for better teaching to lead to the establishment of faculty development offices far removed from the mainstream of instructional activities and staffed by full- or part-time faculty members who were known as "master" teachers before being taken from the classroom for this new assignment. Such efforts are seldom successful, as the faculty members are not trained in instructional design or evaluation. Neither are they familiar with the academic support resources beyond their own fields. Media operations, meanwhile, are increasingly hiring instructional designers who can help faculty articulate learning objectives and design learning experiences that, with the help of the librarian information specialist for that discipline, incorporate existing resources and develop other materials as needed. The interaction of the classroom faculty member, the instructional designer, and the librarian can make for an ongoing dynamic climate for faculty development in which the students are the ultimate benefactors of a learning process that is more individualized and more preparatory for lifelong learning. The difficulty remains in the perception that only classroom faculty members have teaching expertise.

Outreach Opportunities

Institutions that, because of their mission and location, are committed to ongoing work with their surrounding business communities should also consider the potential role of library-based instruction in such activities. At the Auraria Library, the only publicly supported academic library in downtown Denver, a business partnership program was initiated as both a public relations and a fund-raising effort. Although the library was already open to the general public, the program encouraged use of its resources by the business community and offered various levels of discounts for services based on the level of the contributions made by the companies. Most popular among the benefits are seminars for company employees tailored to the informational needs of a particular department. Almost all of the employees are college graduates who had completed their degrees before there was a concern for information literacy. While they may have used the library for a research paper on Shakespeare or a political theory, they never learned how library resources could help them in real-life situations such as determining whether to offer a loan to a local company. The Library Business Partnership Program, therefore, is not only a source of additional funds but is also perceived as a meaningful service of the campus to downtown businesses. Similar seminars could also be built into continuing education programs and alumni reunions that include professional updates.

Summary

The average academic library holds great opportunity for quality nonclassroom learning that can benefit students, faculty, alumni, and the local business community. The major detriments to such learning are limited perceptions of libraries and librarians by campus administrators and the classroom faculty. To change this situation, traditional curriculum-planning avenues must be used so that library-based learning becomes assimilated into overall efforts to offer quality education for the information age.

References

"A Colorado Response to the Information Society: The Changing Academic Library." Conference of the Colorado Commission on Higher Eduction and the Colorado Academic Library Committee, Denver, October 1983. Papers to be made available through the Educational Resources Information Center.
Breivik, P. S. *Open Admissions and the Academic Library*. Chicago: American Library Association, 1977.
Cross, K. P. "Libraries in the Learning Society." Speech made to the Library Instruction Round Table meeting, American Library Association Conference, Dallas, Texas, June 26, 1979.
Horton, F. W., Jr. "Information Literacy vs. Computer Literacy." *American Society of Information Science Bulletin*, 1983, *11* (4), 14–16.
Knapp, P. B. *The Monteith College Experiment*. New York: The Scarecrow Press, 1966.

Newman, F. *Higher Education and the American Resurgence.* Princeton, N.J.: The Carnegie Foundation for the Advancement of Teaching, 1985.

Suput, R. R. "Introduction." In N.Z. Williams and J. T. Tsukamoto (eds.), *Library Instruction and Faculty Development: Growth Opportunities in the Academic Community.* Ann Arbor, Mich.: Pierian Press, 1980.

Patricia Senn Breivik is director of the Auraria Library, which serves over thirty-two thousand students and faculty of the Community College of Denver, the Metropolitan State College, and the University of Colorado at Denver. She was a 1983-1984 American Council on Education Fellow in Academic Administration and since then has been serving part-time as special assistant to the president of the University of Colorado.

Fieldwork is a dynamic learning mode for any school or curriculum willing to make a commitment of imagination and resources.

Field Experience, Practicums, and Internships

Virginia Witucke

Although learning from work has always been a part of life, the move to formal schooling resulted in a reliance on learning from symbols. Periodically, academe rediscovers work in a real-life setting as a mode of learning. Fieldwork has variously been trumpeted as a means of bringing relevance to the ivory tower, a panacea for liberal arts programs, a necessity for professional education, a complement to classroom instruction, a way of developing involved and informed citizens, and a unique and valid way of learning.

Forms

Field-related learning activities range from substitutes for working to jobs for pay. Simulations of various sorts have been developed to bring a sense of reality into the classroom. Laboratory work resembles that done in a job setting. Observations and field trips expose students to real-life situations but require no direct involvement. On-campus courses may include projects requiring hands-on experience in a work setting. Academic courses and independent studies may be field-based. Cross-cultural experiences, such as the junior year abroad or the urban semester, in which the student actually lives in another culture, represent immersion in a nonacademic setting but generally do not emphasize learning through work. Practicums of various sorts, such as internships and student teaching, involve students in work experience arranged for its educational value. Cooperative education programs at best have a strong educational component, as can community service activities. The most realistic type of situation is likely to be the work-study job, which is only incidentally educational.

This chapter will focus on field experiences, practicums, and internships. *Field experience* will be used as the generic term for work assignments performed in an ongoing organizational milieu, arranged by an academic institution as part of its educational program. The experience is shaped to enhance learning, especially through the use of job rotation, coaching, and extensive feedback. The academic institution provides accompanying activities to help the student learn from experience.

Advantages of Field Experience

Those who support fieldwork believe it to be a valid way of meeting academic goals. A fieldworker is exposed to a lot of information, some of it not readily available elsewhere. Thus, classroom and library learning can be extended, clarified, reinforced, and tested. Skills unique to the work setting are learned through instruction, observation, use, and evaluation. Students learn something of the demands and conventions of adult work. More important, skills vital to lifelong learning can result—making hypotheses, gathering data from the milieu, analyzing needs for additional information and finding appropriate resources, synthesizing data, reflecting, and drawing conclusions.

Social and communication skills may be developed or refined. Interrelationships among people and their environments are more clearly seen, and the complexity of life is exemplified. Issues are illuminated. Self-knowledge results from working in a field setting, where strengths, weaknesses, preferences, and gaps in knowledge can be identified. Field experience may help develop values, commitment, social sensitivity, and motivation to learn. Self-reliance, initiative, willingness to take responsibility, and self-esteem increase.

Field experience offers advantages to the academic institution. Placements allow students to specialize or do advanced work, often using labs and equipment unavailable on campus. Field contacts provide continuing education for the faculty and offer opportunities for research. Observing students in another environment gives feedback on the college's program and policies.

Disadvantages

Those who write about field learning strongly support it. This unanimity of opinion is not reflected in academic practice, where fieldwork is not standard. Many faculty members believe fieldwork to be antithetical to intellectualism and an inefficient and ineffective way of learning. Field-based learning can reinforce the status quo, as students learn to emulate rather than to analyze. Fieldwork takes time away from formal education. The potential benefits of field experience are difficult to control; there is no guarantee that learning will result. Furthermore, a great deal of staff time is involved in planning and running field-experience programs (FEPs). Most faculty members lack expertise in dealing with experiential learning, and the academic reward system does not encourage time spent on field experience.

Such benefits and disadvantages should be seriously considered by any faculty examining field-based learning. The remainder of this chapter explores what is involved in organizing and implementing a field-experience program that stresses purposeful learning.

Getting Started

The use of field experience in an institution should have a strong conceptual base, which requires study of program rationales and models, and surveys programs already existing on the campus. This makes possible an educationally valid decision to implement a field experience program and lays the foundation for developing appropriate policies and procedures. Highly recommended readings on values of field learning are those by Cahn (1974), Coleman (1976), Kendall (1983), and Kolb and Fry (1975). The issue has been addressed most recently in the Newman report for the Carnegie Foundation for the Advancement of Teaching ("Excerpts . . .," 1978). *Field Study* (Borzak, 1981) and *Experience and Learning* (Chickering, 1977) are particularly helpful works.

In many ways, setting up or revising an FEP is the same as doing so for any course. Goals and objectives must be stated, general content outlined, course structure devised, amount of credit determined, student eligibility for participation specified, necessary resources identified, and evaluation designed. A decision must also be made about whether field experience will be required or elective.

Scheduling

Where in a student's academic sequence does field experience belong? Although it could represent the culmination of the academic program, it is usually placed at some midpoint, when students can bring learning to their assignment and take their new perspective to the rest of their schooling. Should field experience be offered in the regular school year, in summer, or in intersession? Should participation be scheduled full-time or part-time, or should both options be available? Should work extend over more than one term? If a full-time block during a regular term is used, what changes should be required in the scheduling of other courses? Should full-time assignments be completed over a consecutive period or alternated with classes on campus? Are there any constraints on part-time work? For example, should there be a rotating or a fixed schedule?

Credit

It is inappropriate to offer fieldwork as a learning experience without accrediting that participation. On what basis should credit be determined? Typically, one week of full-time work (thirty-five to forty hours) is equated with one semester hour of credit. Another approach ties credit to accomplishments. For example, the student could be expected to successfully complete a stated project at the field setting and write one position paper to receive a certain number of credits. However, it is fairly difficult to break away from time expectations of some sort.

How much credit should be awarded? Generally it ranges from the equivalent of one course to a full semester, and variable credit is a desirable option. The amount of credit relates to the proportion of a student's total program that can be usefully devoted to fieldwork, balanced against the need for other types of learning and the constraints of program administration.

Ensuring Learning

While simply turning students loose in a work situation undoubtedly affects participants, the quality of learning is not ensured. The most crucial decisions relating to field-experience programs concern its educational value.

Before the Experience Begins. What background should the student bring to fieldwork? While maturity, knowledge, and other characteristics affect readiness, prerequisites are most easily stated in terms of course and credit requirements. Certainly other prerequisites are possible, such as assigned readings or exploratory field visits. Students could be expected to take aptitude or interest inventories useful in planning the assignment. Set up an application process that has educational as well as administrative value. Procedures should be formal and require the applicant to tell why he or she wants to participate. A preliminary proposal for experience might be requested; this encourages students to think in terms of educational goals and to begin assuming responsibility for learning. Use interviews as part of the application process.

How will students be matched with placement sites? Three major approaches have been used—letting students locate their own placements, setting up assignments on an ad hoc basis, and having a pool of potential placements from which students may choose. How should the placement relate to the student's background? Should placement be based on student needs or wants? Will students be able to participate in more than one assignment? Can more than one student be placed at a site at the same time? How frequently can a site be used? Who makes the final placement decision? After the preliminary matching of student and site, participants should get acquainted, share expectations, and test their ability to work together.

What is the content of the fieldwork? What activities are generic to field experience? How will the program for a particular student be developed? If students are to assume responsibility for their own learning, a student-prepared proposal or contract is desirable. This proposal is the equivalent of a course syllabus, but it is developed by the student, with the help of faculty members, site supervisor, and peers. At a minimum, the proposal contains goals and objectives, suggested activities, a tentative schedule, and a means of evaluation. It may include plans for readings, visits to other agencies, and attendance at meetings.

What kinds of fieldwork orientation activities are desirable for the various participants? Workshops, lectures, printed materials, and one-to-one dialogues are the major modes of presentation; simulations, role playing, and day-long immersions on-site have been used for student orientation. Faculty members and field supervisors need to understand program whys and hows, advantages of participation, and their respective roles. Student orientation conveys academic expectations, work habits and ethics, emotional support for students, housekeeping details, and guidance in learning from experience. Orientation must respect participants' limited time, while communicating the information they need.

During the Assignment. Will field participants meet together? If so, how frequently? This may be as often as once a week, plus informal gatherings. What will be the form and content of these sessions? Possible activities are discussions of assignments, reports on related topics, exploration of issues in terms of the respective placements, background lectures, guidance in experiential learning, and remedial instruction. What other activities should accompany field experience? Generally a daily journal of participation is kept, noting activities, intellectual and emotional reactions, questions raised and answered, and personal strengths and weaknesses revealed. Assignments, academic papers, or research studies may be required. Such activities should help students probe beneath the surface of their work, learn more about the nature of inquiry, and see the links between theory and practice. Special projects done to benefit the field placement are valuable in that they give the student some scope for doing independent, original work.

What kinds of feedback will be used? How frequently? All through the field experience the student receives feedback from the environment. A more systematic and explicit feedback should be provided by placement and faculty supervisors on a regularly scheduled basis and as specific needs arise. The field experience must be monitored as it unfolds, to uphold the quality of student work and the experience provided to them. The faculty supervisor should communicate frequently with each student and his or her supervisor, occasionally by visits to the site. Problems that commonly arise are the use of field participants to do clerical or highly repetitive work, to take the place of paid staff, or to do work for which they are inadequately prepared. Student, field supervisor, and faculty supervisor need to regularly review the student's proposal for direction and to revise it as necessary. Since some situations are insoluble, a policy should define the conditions that would cause a field assignment to be terminated.

Identifying Sites

Potential placement sites can be identified through a process of networking—collecting leads from faculty, staff, alumni, and other contacts inside and outside the institution. Other sources are directories such as the *Encyclopedia of Associations*, professional literature, professional associations, community directories (check the public library, United Way, Welcome Wagon, hotlines, hospitals, and government agencies), and the Yellow Pages. Solicit information and volunteers through announcements and advertisements. The campus is a likely placement site, with opportunities for teaching, research, social services, recreational leadership, and administration. How far afield this hunt will go depends on FEP goals, whether the local community can provide placements of the number and type needed, the practicality of sending students off-campus, and the extent of supervision desired. Several schools have set up fieldwork centers at some distance from campus to enlarge the range and number of placements, while providing university supervisory personnel.

Carefully evaluate the resulting pool of organizations. A simple questionnaire or interview will winnow out many unsuitable or unwilling candidates. The remaining organizations should be visited by staff members or their designees to investigate firsthand the potential for sponsoring practicums. For all acceptable sites, basic information such as goals, staffing, types of activities, and facilities should be placed in a file available to students. As well as a pool of placement sites, there is occasionally going to be a need for some ad hoc assignments. And there may be times when it is appropriate for students to propose their own placements. These sites must also be carefully vetted.

Instructors

On-Campus Faculty. Who will staff the FEP? The faculty has an ongoing responsibility for setting up program goals and procedures, advising students, identifying and evaluating placement sites, monitoring the program, and providing consultant help as needed. The demands of coordinating fieldwork require compensated staff time. Faculty members who supervise field assignments in addition to their regular teaching loads find it hard to do justice to both. Using graduate students to oversee assignments is unsatisfactory. They provide no long-term program continuity, have a limited understanding of what is needed to be effective, lack deep commitment to the program, and bring limited general knowledge to their position. Furthermore, using graduate assistants indicates the low esteem in which fieldwork is held.

What level and type of personnel will participate? Campus placement offices may be able to take over that aspect of programs; coordination may be done by administrative and support staff, but the pedagogic activities call for faculty members. Staff members should be chosen according to how their qualities will meet the demands of the program, with participation being voluntary. It may be desirable to bring in new staff members to fulfill this function.

What will be the function of the faculty members assigned to the FEP? They will be program developers, placement specialists, counselors, instructional developers, seminar leaders, work supervisors, consultants, evaluators, coordinators, researchers, and public relations specialists. Specify expectations, especially for supervision, since this is a major role that is often neglected. What configuration of activities (field visits, telephone calls, on-campus consultations, monitoring of student logs) will be used? What is the minimum frequency of contact?

How should teaching load be determined for those working with the FEP, if there is no campus policy? One method is by a formula that equates number of students and length of their participation with the courses. For example, supervising eight students in short-term placements could be considered equivalent to one course. Any formula should consider the amount of individualized contact required, plus time for visits and for instructional planning. Another approach, paying an honorarium for each student supervised, may encourage faculty participation, but it neither creates faculty time nor deals with program planning and coordination. Use stipends when a specialized background is needed or the number of field participants is temporarily too large for the assigned staff. Specify the amount of the stipend and what work is expected for it. Build a substantial amount of lead time into a new program.

On-Site Supervisors. Site supervisors are de facto adjunct faculty. What standards should they be expected to meet and how shall suitability be judged? It is vital that the supervisor be a good role model as well as mentor. Criteria might include training or education (amount, type, quality), extent of relevant work experience in general and at this site, a high enough status in the organization to gain entree for the participant as needed, and involvement in professional organizations. Consider also the prospective supervisor's willingness to take the mentor's role, ability to communicate with the student at the appropriate level, flexibility, and vision. Such qualities are less easily determined, although interviews and visits can reveal some sense of the person's suitability.

What will be expected of site supervisors, and how will they be remunerated? While there are both abstract compensations (for example, a sense of professional contribution) and somewhat less elusive ones like the assistance given by the fieldworker, concrete rewards should be provided. Some options are honorariums, public recognition, and institutional privileges, such as a library card, faculty rates for sports and cultural events, invitations to department programs, and free or reduced tuition.

Evaluation

What kinds of evaluation will be done in the field experience program? Evaluation is threefold, being concerned with the student's learning and performance, the suitability of the placement, and program effectiveness. The goals statement is the obvious starting point in planning the evaluation. If the purpose is to develop sensitivity to people, the means of assessment will be far different than for a program aimed at developing job skills or problem-solving skills. Whatever measures are developed call for before-and-after measurement, so that the impact of the experience can be assessed. Evaluative data may be gathered through observation, work samples, structured interviews, written tests, simulations, role playing, student logs, final reports, and critical incidents that illustrate learning.

Summative evaluation of the placement site is done by all participants. Was the desired experience actually provided? How did the expenditure of resources compare with the results? What aspects of the experience went well? What improvements could be made? Program evaluation looks at the efficiency and effectiveness of all components and how they fit together. Analyze data showing participation, resources used, and impact to determine whether the program is justified, and if so, what changes still need to be made.

How will students be graded? Many schools use a pass-or-fail system, since the student is undertaking such a new experience and has several supervisors. If letter grades are used, define the basis for determining a grade and communicate it to students. While the faculty supervisor assigns the grade, the field supervisor's input to the decision must be clear.

Another aspect of evaluation is its long-term impact. Have the benefits continued over a period of time? Have any unanticipated side effects occurred, such as changes in institutional enrollment or corporate grants? Unfortunately, these relationships are difficult to determine. Nevertheless a field experience program cannot be justified unless it has more than short-lived benefits.

Other Considerations

Documents. The FEP results in various documents—a program manual, administrative forms, and instructional materials. A manual of policies and procedures communicates program intent and structure and is a continuing reference for participants. This chapter has discussed many of the topics that would be included in such a publication. Documents should be dated and periodically revised. Administrative forms help standardize and streamline procedures. Among the more important ones are student applications, evaluation forms, questionnaires or interview schedules for surveying prospective supervisors, and forms describing placement sites. Instructional documents include orientation materials, syllabi, and workbooks or worksheets for student assignments.

Budget. A commitment to student field learning requires money. Besides salaries for professional staff members, the field experience program requires secretarial assistance. Any visits off-campus must be reimbursed at prevailing mileage and per-diem rates. There will be heavy telephone use. If the FEP is not limited to the local community, provide for plenty of long-distance telephoning, including collect calls from field sites. If there is an off-campus center requiring live-in personnel from the main campus, their expenses for the second home are to be underwritten. Research on program effectiveness requires financial support. The formal budget should attempt to anticipate all expenses and put a realistic cost on them.

Public Relations. An effective program is the best publicity there is, but it takes conscious effort to build and strengthen ties with the program's public. The program should be well understood within the academic community, so that it will be morally and financially supported. Faculty and administrators should be informed of program availability and structure; continuing reporting maintains program awareness and documents participation and effectiveness. The FEP should be widely and accurately publicized to students so that they understand the nature and demands of participation and its rewards. Students must be aware of prerequisites, be able to discuss participation with a knowledgeable counselor, and know when and how to apply.

Another major audience for public information consists of the organizations that could sponsor fieldworkers or are already doing so. Besides the program description and role expectations, the advantages and satisfactions of sponsorship should be emphasized. The method of applying to participate should be clearly outlined. It is vital to keep in touch with current and past sponsors, recognizing and encouraging their contributions. Alumni, other funding sources, the local community, and potential employers of the institution's graduates all have reason to be interested in the FEP.

Carrying on the Program

The FEP needs monitoring to ensure that it begins on the right track and stays there. This is likely to be the particular responsibility of a campus committee, which includes representation of nonfaculty participants. Some schools have also used advisory councils, made up of representatives of organizations that sponsor fieldworkers. This committee provides oversight, guidance, and direction. It identifies and deals with unanticipated situations, policies and procedures that prove inappropriate or inadequate, and needs that change. The committee assesses the quality of the program, keeps it from stultifying, and ensures that field-based learning remains useful.

Conclusion

That people learn *something* from work experience is unarguable. That an academic institution can harness and direct this potential has been demonstrated. That it *should* do so is an issue to be answered after careful, prolonged consideration of field-experience demands and rewards. A field program balances great potential for learning against a major expenditure of resources. It requires vision, commitment, flexibility, and persistence. In the short run, field experience enhances academic learning through the use of the outside world and its resources. More important, field experience provides a link to that world in which students are preparing to live as citizens and as individuals.

References

Borzak, L. (ed.). *Field Study: A Sourcebook for Experiential Learning.* Beverly Hills, Calif.: Sage, 1981.
Cahn, S. M. "The Content of a Liberal Education." In S. Hook (ed.), *The Idea of a Modern University.* Buffalo, N.Y.: Prometheus, 1974.
Chickering, A. W. *Experience and Learning: An Introduction to Experiential Learning.* New Rochelle, N.Y.: Change Magazine Press, 1977.
Coleman, J. S. "Differences Between Experiential and Classroom Learning." In M. T. Keeton and Associates, *Experiential Learning: Rationale, Characteristics, and Assessment.* San Francisco: Jossey-Bass, 1976.
"Excerpts from Newman's Report on Higher-Education Policy." *Chronicle of Higher Education,* September 18, 1985, pp. 17–29.
Kendall, J. C. "Values as the Core of Institutional Commitment: Finding a Common Ground." In T. C. Little (ed.), *Making Sponsored Experiential Learning Standard Practice.* New Directions for Experiential Learning, no. 20. San Francisco: Jossey-Bass, 1983.
Kolb, D. A., and Fry, R. "Toward an Applied Theory of Experiential Learning." In C. L. Cooper (ed.), *Theories of Group Processes.* New York: Wiley, 1975.

Virginia Witucke is an instructor and a librarian who participated in field experience during her bachelor's and master's programs. Her dissertation explores the place of library experience in library education. Witucke has taught at Purdue University, University of Iowa, Pratt Institute, University of Arizona, and Northern Illinois University.

While museums and art galleries are a rich source of leisure-time enjoyment, they can also become a focal point for exciting learning programs for the adult student.

Art Galleries and Museums: Nonclassroom Learning for the Nontraditional Student

Ruth Schwartz

Today, more adults than ever are enrolling in art history and art criticism classes offered by continuing education programs of colleges and universities. While art history and art criticism courses are a valid component of programs for traditional students, their popularity with adult learners is exceptional and parallels the increasing popularity of museums themselves.

In 1966 Joseph Allen Patterson, director of the American Association of Museums, stated that the "rate of increase in museum attendance exceeds both the rate of increase of population and the rate of establishment of new museums" (1968, p. 37). In the succeeding twenty years this rate has increased significantly, and special loan exhibitions attract crowds in every major city. Efforts have been made to analyze the relationship between museums and their educational programs, as in the seminal conference held by the Smithsonian Institution at the University of Vermont in 1966. As a paradigm of museums, the Smithsonian Institution has developed the largest noncredit, nonprofit continuing education program in the world. It has been described as the "largest and most sophisticated leisure-time program in the country" (Solinger, 1981). However, the overall educational effort of museums is less than adequate as documented recently by a three-year national study (Commission on Museums for a New Century, 1985), and which by extension can be inferred specifically about art galleries as well. This lack is being addressed to some degree by continuing education programs.

In this and other areas of study, adults are increasingly becoming an important market for higher education institutions, providing not only tuition and fees but, it could also be hoped, eventually political support. According to the *Digest of Educational Statistics 1983-84* (1984), there was an all-time high of 21,252,000 participants in adult education in 1981, representing 12.8 percent of the total adult population in the United States.

Shortened work hours plus longer life spans produce more leisure time, creating the opportunity and enthusiasm to pursue interests in the humanities for which adult education can offer exciting fulfillment. As Bergevin (1967) writes, it is adult education that can provide the "knowledge of what to do culturally and spiritually with our lives and talents" (p. 11). Most adults want programs that do not require them to participate continuously. They may come for one course, for several years, or, increasingly, they continue indefinitely as long as new options are available.

Building a Successful Course

The key to the success of these courses is to keep them clearly focused on the interests of the participants. Unlike many traditional courses, the emphasis should be placed on the personal growth of individuals as opposed to the memorization of facts regarding particular artists or art movements. As suggested by Johansen (1979), "The most significant reward of developing one's ability to appreciate works of art is increased depth of personal experience rather than increased ability to rank visual entities" (p. 12). With this as the objective in discussions and lectures, the focal point for presentations must center around why a work of art affects one in a certain manner. Descriptions of the form and the explanation of the meaning of the work then become the background to stimulate thought concerning the "why."

Lectures, therefore, should be presented with the goal of learning to appreciate works of art in increasingly greater depth. It is through explanation of interrelationships that participants are introduced to paintings and other art forms in their broader social, cultural, and historical contents. This is accomplished by following the concept of art appreciation described by Ingarden (1973) as a process of three different phases: the first with the viewer focusing on a particular work as a whole, the second with the viewer focusing on the work's parts and their linkage, and the third with a refocusing on the work as a whole.

To many, the complex collections of a museum or gallery are bewildering in and of themselves. Where to start? How to look? What to see? This is where preparatory slide presentations and subject discussions followed by on-site museum or art gallery experiences can create an effective package of learning as well as provide experiences in how to approach complex exhibits in a meaningful way. The use of slides combined with visits to museums and galleries expands the teaching of the history and appreciation of art, serving the purpose of giving the viewer some prior understanding of what Lankford (1984) terms *relevant critical dialogue*. While the use of slides to present a work of art on the screen can give learners only an approximation of the three-dimensional quality of the work of art, the slides do serve to give them the opportunity to concentrate on that work of art no matter what its size; frequently this can be done by focusing on details as well. This facilitates the ease of further introduction of slides of related art works to make comparisons or to create a context. Some educators, such as Banfield (1982), disparage the use of slides, stating that the differences between original works of art and slides is considerable. This criticism, however, loses its validity when the slides are combined with actual viewings of the pieces being studied.

The size of the class will to a great degree dictate the pedagogical method to be used. A large group of fifty to seventy-five students almost always mandates a complete lecture approach, with questions encouraged only at the end. This is true also of visits to view particular works of art; the size of the group determines the amount of lecture-question interaction possible. In smaller groups of fifteen to twenty-five adults, it is the role of the lecturer to ask leading questions and to make direct statements to refine learners' levels of appreciation. This can easily be accomplished by requesting relevant background information of the participants at the first class meeting.

Accessibility must be considered in the planning of museum and art gallery courses, and here institutions located in culturally rich urban areas have a considerable advantage insofar as the number and range of courses that can be offered. Excursions can include a single museum or gallery visit, or they can be extended to include lunch with an afternoon visit to another site. It is advisable to visit one museum per time frame for an on-site lecture, or to emphasize one particular historical period and visit two or three galleries. While this may seem like simple common sense, its implication for art education is significant, since the learning experience cannot be effective when too broad an area is covered or when the range of items is too extensive. Related items of interest in other departments of a museum can, of course, be introduced during a lecture.

The planning of the visits must be very carefully done. Such factors as attention span and physical endurance must be considered. Because of the effort required to view a work of art intensively, it is possible for the viewer to become too exhausted to derive any pleasure or knowledge from the work. When there is public transportation or when adults have private transportation, it is easier for participants to meet at the museum or gallery. If a sufficient number prefer bus transportation and are willing to pay the costs, the institution should, with due consideration for adequate insurance coverage, make such arrangements. In the determination of all logistics, enough flexibility should exist to tailor decisions to the capabilities and interests of the majority or to allow options to accommodate differences.

Particularly when a program is being initiated, it is important to ensure adequate funds to enable the continuing education office to effectively advertise the courses being offered. Eventual word-of-mouth promotion of successful programs can be anticipated.

Taking Classes Abroad

A natural extension to an art history program is a trip abroad to view works of art that could otherwise only be known through slides or photographs, and to experience firsthand the cultural and historical context of the art. The locale for such art tours can be a single country or more, depending on the number of attractions available in the host country and the days allotted to the tour. Planning should start a year in advance to allow time for researching and selecting the sites to be visited, for planning the skeleton itinerary, and for arrangements to be made.

The role of the local travel agent is crucial. Working from the suggested itinerary furnished by the instructor, the agent must select, often through competitive proposals, the country tour agent who will be responsible for on-site arrangements. The foreign tour agent will help refine the itinerary by scheduling sufficient time for planned visits; advising on museum hours and the accessibility of special attractions; arranging local guides, transportation, hotels, and meals; and coping with the myriad details inherent in a specialized group tour. Stays of at least two nights in the same hotel are recommended as being least wearying to adult tour participants; longer stays are preferred if the city can serve as the central base for days trips to selected areas.

Successful art tours will include a variety of art experiences in addition to museum visits. An orientation tour by bus of each new city, with architectural and historical background presented by a local guide, is desirable to provide a more personal base for understanding the culture and art of the region. A bus and driver and foreign guide should be provided for the duration of each visit.

All of the tour's activities must be carefully planned to take into consideration national holidays, local museum hours, and so on. The variety could include art galleries, private collections (arrangements to be made well in advance), churches, cathedrals, and castles. Stops can be arranged at single monuments or to view single altarpieces. Although a full day's agenda is important, it is advisable to return several hours before dinner to allow for shopping and individual exploration. While it is not necessary for all members of the group to be together constantly, and while some members may elect to go off on their own, the tour must maintain its spirit as an educational experience and not a shopping adventure.

The costs of a tour abroad should be all-inclusive, covering, in addition to air and ground transportation, porterage and transfers, continental breakfasts, arranged luncheons at special stops and dinners at restaurants other than the hotel dining room. Gratuities for bus drivers, city guides, and the assigned foreign tour guide should be included and the sums set aside, leaving participants free to enjoy the tour without worrying about tipping too much or too little. Once the costs are computed, the institution sponsoring the trip can add whatever overhead charges are appropriate. Overhead charges should include ample funds for publicizing the tour, particularly until a reputation for the program is built and a satisfied clientele can be expected both to return for additional trips and to recommend the trip to others.

Evaluating Courses

Since adults who pursue art appreciation programs do so not for credit or for a better employment position but for personal enrichment, the success of art programs can be measured by the number of adults who return for the next series of classes. The theme of each course must change in order to maintain interest over a number of years (my current class has had some of the same students for more than fifteen years). If a course is fulfilling, participants recommend it to others; the word-of-mouth endorsements create a pool of prospective adult students who replenish the number lost through normal attrition. More immediate feedback useful to evaluate the suitability of a professor just beginning to offer such courses and to refine the approach and logistics being used can be obtained by the use of an informal survey at the end of the course. Answers to such questions as "Has this class changed your perception or attitudes toward the world about you? If so, in what way?" will be sufficient to learn whether the class is a winner or if a problem exists. Other questions can elicit information useful to planning further courses.

Course Benefits

To the participants the benefits are personal. Their lives are enhanced by deriving a sense of the richness of mankind's artistic and historical culture. They gain simple benefits such as moving into a new area and meeting people with similar interests, visiting museums and galleries that they have been reluctant to visit on their own, traveling in the United States and abroad with a direction for their activities. They derive further personal benefits that come with the pleasure of learning; "the pleasure of testing one's own understanding, and a sense of connection with other people's experiences, perceptions, and creative acts" (Knox, 1981, p. 26).

The institution also benefits. In addition to the immediate financial gains, the awareness by this group of adults of the availability of nontraditional courses can open the door to participation by other special-interest segments of that growing market of adults with leisure time. These programs also foster ongoing course attendance by a growing number of nontraditional students. Positive feelings of continuing education participants could also be cultivated for institutional development efforts. In some cases, the institution may be able to channel underutilized faculty members into such continuing education programs, which in turn could lead to institutional growth. As Steitz (1985, p. 15), says: "Accommodating adult students within higher education provides an institution, staff, and professors an opportunity to examine basic issues such as the nature and purpose of higher education, the social and community role of educational institutions, and academic isolation."

Summary

There is an increasing market for continuing education courses in art history and art criticism, particularly for colleges and universities in urban areas whose mission includes a commitment to nontraditional students. Such courses must be consciously constructed to meet the expectations of adult learners for personal growth, and careful, detailed planning is required to handle the myriad of logistical details involved in creating courses, whether offered locally or abroad. Well-executed programs can look forward to a continuing and growing clientele and may facilitate growth in other areas of the continuing education program.

References

Banfield, E. "Art Versus Collectibles." *Harpers*, 1982, *265* (1587), 28-34.
Bergevin, E. C. *A Philosophy for Adult Education*. New York: Seabury Press, 1967.
Commission on Museums for a New Century. *Museums for a New Century*. Washington, D.C.: American Association of Museums, 1985.
Digest of Educational Statistics 1983-84. Washington, D.C.: National Center for Education Statistics, 1984.
Ingarden, R. "The Structure of Appreciation." In M. Lipman (ed.), *Contemporary Aesthetics*. Boston: Allyn and Bacon, 1973.
Johansen, P. "An Art Appreciation Teaching Model for Visual Aesthetic Education." *Studies in Art Education*, 1979, *20* (3), 4-14.
Knox, A. B. "Adults as Learners." *Museum News*, 1981, *59* (5), 24-29.

Lankford, E. L. "A Phenomenological Methodology for Art Criticism." *Studies in Art Criticism*, 1984, *25* (3), 151-158.

Patterson, J. A. "Museum Programs in Education." In E. Larrabee (ed.), *Museums and Education*. Washington, D.C.: Smithsonian Institution Press, 1968.

Solinger, J. "The Smithsonian Resident Associate Program: A Different Species of Continuing Education." *Continuum*, 1981, *46* (1), 13-18.

Steitz, J. A. "Issues of Adult Development Within the Academic Environment." *Lifelong Learning: The Adult Years*, 1985, *8* (6), 15-18.

Ruth Schwartz is presently university librarian at Fairleigh Dickinson University, Rutherford, N.J. She has been teaching adults art history for over twenty years, integrating with her courses group art tours abroad.

Student activities that are well planned and implemented enhance both the richness of educational experiences and the student retention rate.

Learning Through Student Activities

Susan A. Morrell, Richard C. Morrell

The research and theories on student develoment advanced during the 1960s and 1970s helped define roles and educational purposes for student services personnel of the era. Today, the research and theories continue to develop. But, because of declining enrollment and less federal aid being given to higher education student services, practitioners, researchers, and executive administrators are realizing the value that student activities have in regard to satisfaction in the educational experience, persistence to graduation, and alumni support. In this chapter the benefits of learning through student activities will be discussed in terms of enhancement of recruitment and retention efforts and campus development programs. Initially, however, given the current concern for quality in education, we will discuss the educational potential of such nonclassroom learning and provide a description of the training and evaluation components necessary to ensure quality learning experiences through student activities.

Effects of Activities Participation on Students

The types of learning experiences best provided through student activities have to do primarily with interpersonal skills development and abilities to work effectively within organizational settings. They address the quality concerns that have been raised in regard to active learning that will prepare students for risk taking and citizen participation (Newman, 1985).

Berman (1978) indicates that involvement in student activities and organizations teaches students about group processes, decision making, organizational and administrative skills, budgeting and accounting, and bureaucratic and programming skills. Astin (1977) found that organizational participation positively influences satisfaction with social life and instruction. Participation in formal, organized activities enhances the maturity of students, helps them gain management skills, and facilitates career decision making according to Winter and others (1981). Studies examining the influence that holding a student leadership position has on life satisfaction indicates that the cocurricular involvement of students is positive in the areas of personal development, societal concerns, cultural awareness, and social skills development (Ross-Powers, 1980). A study of fraternity and sorority members found that membership in the Greek system increases self-esteem, conservative views, and social skills (Feldman and Newcomb, 1969). Astin also found that involvement in student government increases self-esteem and satisfaction with friendships. Downey and others (1984) found in a study of former student government leaders that those students who reported that activities contributed to skills improvement reported high levels of satisfaction with social activities and current jobs.

Student activities and organizations provide the opportunity for skill and personal development in the areas of social interaction, management of resources and people, and planning and coordination of projects or programs. Social interaction is developed through both group-theory training from the professional staff and personal experiences. Decision-making skills, budgeting, and committee supervision are all areas that may be developed and learned through managing resources and people in the group. Planning and implementing programs or projects may include learning how to manipulate the bureaucracy, planning and budgeting weeks in advance, negotiating with talent agencies, understanding contracts, using various forms of promotion, recruiting volunteers, writing articles, accounting for ticket receipts or application fees, and understanding how to use audiovisual equipment. Whatever the activity, such opportunities provide unique learning experiences that are difficult to replicate in the classroom. To maximize the positive effects of such experiences, however, requires competent student services personnel who can provide leadership in creating an environment that promotes participation and limits the initial high risks of failure.

Methods for Effective Training

Good learning experiences do not just happen either within the classroom or without. Carefully planned training programs are of primary importance in successful learning-based student activities. There are several techniques for promoting the learning of leadership skills. One of the most frequently used is the formal student leadership training program. This could include a week-long retreat (on- or off-campus), a credit or noncredit course, weekly seminars before or after business meetings, various day-long workshops with guest speakers, and a wide range of educational sessions on student leadership and programming. A typical format for a training program would include an overview of the group's policies, constitution and procedures, team-building exercises, budget examination, introduction of key university or college personnel, initiation into specific office procedures that the group will need to know (equipment operation, purchasing procedures, and so on), and goal and objective setting for the year ahead. Often there will be a training manual or leadership handbook to use for reference throughout the training and later to use as a reference tool for reminding students of the "how to's."

In order to allow for the best use of time and resources and to ensure that all students have the same training and information, formal training should begin by having all members of the group participate. Proper training allows students to understand college policies and ritual, thus making them better informed for decision making. At the conclusion of training, the members set goals and objectives together to keep the group focused throughout the year. When new policies are needed or when crucial decisions must be made, having completed the goals will pay dividends. One of the greatest advantages of formal training is the opportunity for team building to take place. Specific activities should be planned to help the group socialize, learn about each other's personalities, and begin to feel comfortable with one another. This interaction is vital in developing the group harmony that is the basis of a positive learning experience.

The disadvantages of formal training have to do with costs. A week or weekend off-campus retreat is usually expensive, as it must include lodging, meals, and transporation. Even training programs held on-campus may become expensive if meals and room rentals are involved. The costs and staff time spent on printing leadership materials and handbooks and the cost of taking time away from the office must also be considered. Although there are disadvantages, almost all colleges utilize some form of this training.

Another method of student leadership development is informal on-the-job training programs. This training program typically includes individual meetings with student leaders to assist them in learning individual task skills and in learning their role in group processes. Students learn by actually doing the project or task, whether it is writing an editorial column, coordinating student elections, or promoting Greek rush. These experiences teach the students new skills and improve existing ones. They also benefit from individual evaluations of projects and training that are specific to their areas of interest and responsibility. This is an important training method because students are able to develop close working relationships with advisers who may eventually become mentors. Since each student is individually trained, a large commitment of student personnel time is required; and providing for adequate staffing may strain a limited budget. Another potential disadvantage is that the student adviser must rely on the student to inform him or her if questions or problems arise.

A third training technique is the development of written contracts that outline the responsibilities involved in each student position. These contracts are developed by using job descriptions, performance standards, officer responsibility agreements, and a formal evaluation procedure. All contracts should be developed and mutually agreed on by all members of the student group. Performance evaluations should be processed on a peer and adviser level. The objective is to identify behavior patterns that should be modified or reinforced in order to enhance student performance. This technique has proven to be very effective in producing positive change in students. The contracts are individually written and provide the student with the opportunity to begin a learning experience at his or her own skill level. In addition, the contracts generally call for frequent individual review of progress with the student. This provides valuable and timely feedback to both adviser and the student.

Internships, assistantships, and practicums are the fourth technique used to assist students in out-of-classroom learning experiences. Students have the advantage of getting on-the-job experiences and benefitting from an outside evaluation by the practicum supervisor as well as the classroom instructor.

All of these methods of training are being used today, and the methods work best when used in combination with one another. At the University of Northern Colorado (UNC), formal retreat training has been instituted for student government, student publications staff, the student programming board, and Greek umbrella groups. In addition, student handbooks have been or are in the process of being developed to assist the students in procedural operations. These handbooks also include job descriptions and methods of evaluation. Informal training is used to better assist the students in fulfilling their specific responsibilities. In some instances weekly meetings are held with officers or committee coordinators to ensure complete program planning and implementation. Honorary student groups sponsor leadership workshops and seminars, and the campus activities office has developed a program for internships and practicums as well as funding a half-time graduate assistantship position. At UNC a commitment has been made to continuous training for out-of-classroom learning experiences; it is seen as one of the keys to the successful development of its students.

Measurement for Student Development

Brown and others (1979) propose that higher education should adopt a more systematic method of advising, assessing, and recording student activities participation through the use of a student development transcript. Such transcripts contain records of students' personal development and involvements as well as their academic accomplishments. They further suggest that student development transcripts are beneficial to both colleges and students. They stimulate interaction among faculty, staff, and students and provide students with a chart of development that can be used in self-evaluation and life planning; in addition they serve as a record of competencies achieved throughout college experiences. Brown and others further suggest that this documentation could take on a variety of forms—an experimental checklist, a competency-based checklist, a portfolio, or a combination thereof. The experimental checklist would include a statement of experiences or activities that would contribute to the attainment of selected goals. The initial list would be developed by the faculty or the staff, with the student choosing from those activities, or the list could be created by the student in consultation with the faculty or the adviser. Examples of activities might be: attend an international film, work at a day-care center, belong to the debate club, write an article for the school newspaper, or sign up for the tech crew for the homecoming show. These activities could then be grouped into categories such as social, recreational, cultural, and spiritual or just listed as activities that are intended to guide the student along a developmental route (Baier, 1982).

This experimental checklist transcript would ideally be used in conjunction with an advising or mentoring program in which students discuss their developmental goals with an adviser. The advisers may be faculty members or student affairs professionals. Students participate in the activities listed, and the advisers and students check them off when goals have been completed and retain the records for further planning or future personal use such as job placement. This transcript would be primarily a record of involvements and not a measurement of skills or competencies.

The competency-based checklist would contain a listing of proficiencies or skills that students would be able to achieve through participation in campus activities or organizations. As an example, a student may wish to be able to speak effectively in front of a group or effectively run a meeting. Goal setting for competencies would be done with the assistance of advisers, and as competencies were mastered they would be initialed by advisers on the transcripts. To make the student development transcript functional, the idea must be supported by students, student activity advisers, and academic advisers and faculty. Student activity advisers must work with the students to plan participation in student activities that complement the academic curriculum. Concurrently, academic advisers must be willing to support student participation in campus activities. The burden of coordinating the academic and activities curriculum must not rest solely on the student. As needed, the academic and activities advisers should meet jointly and discuss the entire curriculum with the advisees.

A third format of the student development transcript is the portfolio. Students collect data that would serve as a record of their activities, accomplishments, skills, and projects. It might include leadership-training experiences, samples of writings, reports or programs, creative promotional samples, letters of thanks, and testimonials of skills achievements. The portfolio may or may not include a measure of skills competencies allowing reviewers to determine students' levels of achievement. The portfolio could also contain one of the checklists just mentioned, allowing specific goal planning with the samples acting as proof of students' listed competencies and achievements (Baier, 1982).

Institutions implementing student development transcript programs are on the increase at the University of Nebraska, the Univeristy of Iowa, and the University of North Dakota, to name a few. They perfect and polish their ongoing efforts in activities transcripts and mentoring projects. The University of Nebraska maintains the Student Development Mentoring-Transcript Clearinghouse, which collects information on such programs. Information may also be obtained from the National Association for Campus Activities resource library maintained in Columbia, South Carolina.

For a college or university, the benefits of administering a transcript program are numerous. Such a program can increase interaction among faculty, students, and staff and increase awareness of cocurricular activities. It also can increase student utilization of support services and cocurricular programs and can be used as a tool for assessing personal growth. It could become part of the permanent record of student involvements and achievements that might be used for job placement (Baier, 1982). Results of a national survey conducted by Bryan and others (1981) suggest that the cocurricular transcript is preferred by employers over the traditional resume. There was also support for including the transcript with student placement credentials and even stronger support for including some measure of competencies and skills gained as a result of the student's involvement in cocurricular activities. Bryan and others (1981) suggest that employers prefer the experimental checklist because they are able to evaluate students' experiences themselves instead of relying on the faculty or staff to do it. Many of these same business people indicated that they would use the transcript in the interview, since it would provide a basis for discussion about students' competencies.

The type of transcript is not the crucial aspect of this concept, rather the direct advising and assessment of students and their accomplishments are the most important components of any student development transcript program.

Trends in Student Activities Staffing

Persons recruited to work in the area of student activities must be committed to and capable of good teaching, since most of their time will be spent dealing with the issues, problems, and joys of helping students achieve the skills needed to become effective and responsible leaders. Well-qualified entry-level professionals usually have previous student leadership experience and a bachelor's degree; in some instances a master's degree is preferred. Persons applying for activities director must usually have a master's degree and from three to five years of experience working in student activities. Preferred degrees usually include student personnel, counseling, business, and recreation.

Organizations such as the National Association for Campus Activities, the Association for College Unions International, the National Association for College and University Residence Halls, regional interfraternity, and Panhellenic organizations sponsor formal training programs. These organizations draw from the leadership of the profession in their respective areas to present educational seminars, workshops, and extended intensive training programs for student leaders and activities advisers. Such continuing education opportunities are particularly important for student services personnel in settings in which they have little access to other professionals in their field.

In the past student government was a function of the dean's office. Greek affairs had its own office, and student programming was the primary responsibility of the activities adviser. As enrollments continue to decline and budgets decrease, the activities director, like other university administrators, is becoming more of a generalist. In the activities field the trend is for all major student activities and organizational programs and services to be under the leadership of the same director. Assuming that there are enough support personnel, the advantages of this structure are increased communications and collaboration between the student groups, better utilization of staff and financial resources, consistent training for all student organizations, and a single location at which students may inquire about involvement opportunities and activities.

University organizational structures vary as to whom the activities director will report to. Programming boards are usually housed in the student union, and a considerable amount of the student union's programming is also held within the building. This would suggest that the activities adviser should work with the staff in the union under the union director. However, student government is usually closely associated with the chief student affairs office along with Greek affairs, and therefore, it would seem that the director should report to the chief student affairs officer. Both structures are viable and are used throughout the collegiate community. In either case, if the director is responsible for both student government and programming, it is crucial that he or she develop positive working relationships with both the union staff and the student affairs division.

Funding Issues

Student activities are traditionally funded through student activity fees that are collected with tuition. These are either direct line-item allocations or student committee recommended allocations. As part of the fiscal process, student groups submit budgets for consideration and approval by the activities director or the student finance committee in order to receive funding. Besides being necessary for the budgeting process, this method also plays an educational role in teaching the student leaders responsible spending.

There are some key issues that arise frequently in planning student group funding; whether to pay student officers or to keep them volunteer positions, how much travel money should be allocated to student leaders, and whether or not fees should be spent on alcohol and private social functions for the group. Another frequently discussed issue is determining who should have a vote in the student fee allocation process. Should it be a committee or staff, faculty, and students or a committee of students only? (Since athletics, intramurals, and the health services are usually funded by student fees, the professionals in those areas normally try to maintain a faculty-staff influence.) And finally, should the campus activities office be funded through the university budget, student fees, student organizations, or the union budget? There are no fundamentally right or wrong solutions or prescriptions to these issues. Each campus has its own philosophy, and answers to these and many other questions may be restricted to some degree by state or local regulations. Within the varying operational parameters, however, student input in funding decisions allows students to be a part of the university process, to have a say in how their money is spent, and to have experiences in decision making and financial management.

Impact on the Institution

Activities participation can be a positive means of recruiting and retaining students as well as fostering positive memories and feelings for future alumni to communicate to others. Moreover, those who were involved in campus activities and organizations will usually be dedicated to the university after graduation, including offering financial support.

Those student organizations that recruit members early can assist the admissions office through personal mailings and visits to high schools. The fraternities and sororities can be the admission director's best resource, since these volunteers must maintain certain membership levels in order to survive. Other student groups, such as ambassador programs, may volunteer to visit high schools or give university tours. Program boards in conjunction with the residence halls may sponsor high school senior weekends to help recruit students. For those high school students who were active on the student newspaper, student council, or sports programs, a special invitation from program boards or residence halls to visit might convince seniors to apply for admission. In addition, those students who find life enjoyable on campus will stay to graduate and encourage their siblings, friends, and eventually their offspring to attend.

There is a considerable body of research that documents student activities and development as contributing to student retention. Astin (1975) reports that campus involvement and organized living groups were associated with greater than average retention. McGrath (1970) suggests that one benefit of student participation in campus decision making is the student's recognition of the importance of education to the student's future. Beal and Noel (1980) surveyed over one thousand colleges and concluded that inadequate extracurricular activities and inadequate counseling support systems are the two major contributors to student attrition. They also found that positive factors in student retention were a caring attitude toward students, high-quality teaching and advising, and student involvement on campus (Baier, 1982). Through participation in organized student activities, students became more aware of the educational environment and learning opportunities available to them. Activities give more meaning to students' lives and thereby allow them to identify objectives and long-range goals (Williams and Winston, 1985). Activities tend to increase student satisfaction, thus leading to higher student retention rates. Ross-Powers (1980) cites two studies that support this claim. During the mid 1970s Jean Danels conducted a study on student retention as part of her master's thesis for Cornell University. It showed that students involved in cocurricular activities successfully completed college in four years more often than the uninvolved students. Similarly, in 1980 a study by Ed Meyers of St. Cloud University concluded that not being involved in student organizations or not having any peer relationships was identified as one of the seven factors that increased the dropout rate.

Institutions can also benefit financially from students' participation in student activities. Fraternities often raise money for scholarships, and the program boards host big-name entertainers. Activities bring the university attention through the outstanding achievements of the student leaders, which in turn can sometimes be used to foster financial support from the community. Based on experiences of alumni offices and the attendance of alumni at special reunions and university functions, there is some indication of a correlation between student involvement and alumni support. This is also indicated in the Greek system through alumni support of housing functions and scholarships.

Summary

Campus activities and organizations offer learning experiences primarily through interpersonal skills development and organizational processes, although the possibilities for intentional, specific learning is unlimited. The advantages of a well-developed and educationally directed student activities program are clearly supported by the research on the topic, particularly in the area of student retention and increased satisfaction with college experiences. Institutions concerned with such outcomes will want to consider developing well-planned activities programs that include student leadership training and one or more means of documenting students' experiences.

References

Astin, A. W. *Preventing Students from Dropping Out.* San Francisco: Jossey-Bass, 1975.

Astin, A. W. *Four Critical Years: Effects of College on Beliefs, Attitudes, and Knowledge.* San Francisco: Jossey-Bass, 1977.

Baier, J. L. "Measuring Student Development." *Student Activities Programming,* 1982, *14* (8), 30-34.

Beal, P., and Noel, L. *What Works in Student Retention?* Boulder, Colo.: The American College Testing Program, National Center for Higher Education Management System, 1980.

Berman, W. F. "Student Activities and Student Development." *National Association of Student Personnel Administrators Journal,* 1978, *16* (2), 52-54.

Brown, R., Baier, L., Baack, J., Wright, D., and Sanstead, M. "Implications of Student, Parent, and Administrator Attitudes for Implementing a Student Development Transcript." *Journal of College Student Personnel,* 1979, *20* (5), 385-392.

Bryan, W. T., Mann, R. B., and North, R. A. "The Cocurricular Transcript—What Do Employers Think? A National Survey." *National Association of Student Personnel Administrators Journal,* 1981, *19* (1), 29-36.

Downey, R. G., Bosco, P. J., and Silver, E. M. "Long-Term Outcomes of Participation in Student Government." *Journal of College Student Personnel,* 1984, *25* (3), 245-250.

Feldman, K. A., and Newcomb, T. M. *The Impact of College on Students.* San Francisco: Jossey-Bass, 1969.

McGrath, E. J. *Should Students Share the Power?* Philadelphia: Temple Press, 1970.

Newman, F. *Higher Education and the American Resurgence.* Princeton, N.J.: The Carnegie Foundation for the Advancement of Teaching, 1985.

Ross-Powers, S. J. "Co-curricular Activities Validated Through Research." *Student Activities Programming,* 1980, *13* (6), 46-48.

Williams, M., and Winston, R. B., Jr. "Participation in Organized Student Activities and Work: Differences in Developmental Task Achievement of Traditional-Aged College Students." *National Association of Student Personnel Administrators Journal,* 1985, *22* (3), 52-59.

Winter, D. G., McClelland, D. C., and Stewart, A. J. *A New Case for the Liberal Arts: Assessing Institutional Goals and Student Development.* San Francisco: Jossey-Bass, 1981.

Susan A. Morrell is the director of campus activities and student organizations at the University of Northern Colorado and serves as regional coordinator for the Heart of America Region of the National Association of Campus Activities.

Richard C. Morrell is currently a doctoral student at the University of Northern Colorado. Previously, he had been employed by the Office of Residential Life at Emporia State University, in Kansas.

The higher education literature discusses the ability of nonclassroom learning to respond to the needs of individual learners. It also discusses the special considerations of nonclassroom learning for implementation, funding, and evaluation.

Nonclassroom Learning: A Review of the Literature

Jo Ann Carr

In *Three Thousand Futures* (1980) the Carnegie Council on Policy Studies in Higher Education identifies major axes that will influence the development of higher education for the remainder of this century. These key issues of "greater equality of access to higher education for minorities, women, and adults"; innovation; and "greater environmental impact on higher education" (p. 7) echo the concerns that are cited in the literature of nonclassroom learning.

Why Nonclassroom Learning?

The Commission on Nontraditional Study (1973) has defined nontraditional education as "an attitude that puts the student first and the institution second, concentrates more on the former's need than on the latter's convenience, encourages diversity of individual opportunity, and deemphasizes time and space or even course requirements in favor of competence, and where applicable, performance" (p. 6). This attitude is a major impetus for the development of many forms of nonclassroom learning.

Quinn and Sellars (1974) cite Dunnivant's identification of "relevance, meaningfulness, and action" as the "cue words of college students" in their discussion of the role of students in field experience education. Quinn and Sellars's own definition of the student as "an initiator, problem solver, and decision maker; cultural analyst and strategist; interactor, information source, and network developer; free agent; value clarifier; communicator; and recipient" (p. 37) is a further explication of the activist consumer student identified in *Three Thousand Futures* (Carnegie Council on Policy Studies in Higher Education, 1980).

The National Institute of Education's Study Group on the Conditions of Excellence in American Higher Education (1984) also stresses the need for "student involvement, high expectations, and feedback" as the "three critical conditions of excellence" (p. 17). Later in the report, the study group states that "a mix of teaching styles can be an effective device for increasing involvement" (p. 27). The ability of learning technologies to provide more personal contact between students and faculty is also noted. This closer interaction with students and the necessity of nonclassroom learning to be participative will provide an opportunity to give greater attention to the passive or reticent student.

The need for students' involvement in their own learning was earlier identified by the Carnegie Commission on Higher Education in their 1972 report on instructional technology. In that report the commission asserted that "the new technology will also tend to draw instruction from the historical requirements-met-through-teaching approach to a resources-available-for-learning approach" (p. 2). This new emphasis will dictate that students be more active in their own education and be able to deal with greater flexibility and variety in their education. While predicting that, by the year 2000, 10 to 20 percent of instruction on-campus and a minimum of 80 percent of off-campus instruction will utilize instructional technology, the commission cautions that technology should only be used when appropriate. Technology should be used when the teaching-learning task is "essential to the course of instruction" and when "the task . . . could not be performed as well—if at all—for the students served without the technology contemplated" (p. 11). Faculty members would also benefit from the introduction of technology both by the introduction of competition and by a reduction of routine instructional responsibilities.

This benefit to faculty is just one of many cited by Welling (1983) in his discussion of the role of telecommunications in enabling higher education to respond to changing demands and opportunities. The flexibility of time and place for learning; the ability of technology to "extend access to limited human resources," as well as to "encourage interinstitutional cooperation and resource sharing" (p. 34) were also noted.

The pervasiveness of telecommunications in higher education was indicated by Tate and Kressel (1983) in citing Dirr's 1981 Higher Education Utilization Study. This study revealed that 61 percent of the 2,293 colleges and universities surveyed were using television for instruction. Tate also cites Dirr's finding that there are one hundred thousand informal learners for each enrolled student, which demonstrates the ability of technology to generate goodwill.

Implementation

In *The Fourth Revolution,* the Carnegie Commission on Higher Education (1972) recommends that responsibility for the introduction and use of instructional technology be placed at the highest administrative level. This recommendation is also a key component of Stephenson and Sexton's (1974) principles for the successful implementation of an experiential learning program. Based on their experience at the University of Kentucky, Stephenson and Sexton caution that "success in bringing about change is always a mixture of calculated strategy and dumb luck" (p. 56). Nevertheless, they identify the essential conditions for successful implementation: "Use influentials and elites, timing, communications management, and be consistent with existing norms and objectives" (p. 56). In addition to these general guidelines, Ramsey (1974) identifies some unique factors that must be considered when implementing field experience education. The dual role of field experience supervisors is noted as well as the environmental and student characteristics that influence the success of the program. Ramsey recognizes the four structures for field experience programs: the student as an employee, honored guest, special assistant, and project-oriented structure.

The need to reward the field project supervisor is also recognized by Van Aalst (1974) in his discussion of program design. He later cites the need to determine academic credit for special learning experiences as a major issue in implementation. In summarizing the process of implementation, O'Connell and Moomaw (1974) define the five stages of implementation as "instigate, introduce, interpret, implement, and continuously inspect the undertaking" (p. 85). External influence or outside agents often play the role of instigator in the experience of O'Connell and Moomaw.

In their study of nontraditional degree programs in California, Illinois, and New York, Bowen and others (1979) determined that nontraditional programs are initiated at organizational levels above the campus. Their study also examined the bases for decision making within policy areas for those involved in nontraditional programs. Feeney and Riley (1975) emphasize the need for a broader range of faculty competence as a major implementation issue in their discussion of learning contracts at New College, Sarasota. They further state that "an institution must be able to tolerate the pluralism that a contract system requires" (p. 28).

In her study of twenty-four North Dakota faculty members involved in off-campus experiences, Johnson (1985) also identifies special faculty requirements for program implementation. Faculty members need more time for class preparation, as they need to compensate for the lack of resources and to deal with the logistics of setting up an instructional location. The tendency of off-campus students to be less tolerant of inadequate teaching and to wish to use their professional experiences as a basis for learning also requires more time for intellectual preparation for the off-campus faculty.

Costs and Funding

Bowen and others have noted that "the development of budgeting measures for nontraditional programs is currently in its very initial stages" (1979, p. 100). However, their study also indicates that budgetary decision making for nontraditional programs "appeared to be more closely related to qualitative policy and program factors than is the case with budgetary decisions concerning traditional programs" (p. 100). In five of nine programs studied there was no quantitative justification for their establishment. In addition to identifying some special costs associated with nonclassroom programs, Bowen and others argue that the special attention given by state fiscal agencies to new programs provides an excellent opportunity for the development of an improved relationship. In developing this relationship and in determining financing needs, they recommend that the following questions be asked:

1. How do nontraditional students finance their education? How do funding arrangements influence enrollment?
2. What are the initial and operating costs of different program components?
3. How do current budgetary practices impede development and support?
4. What is the state's return on its investment?

In their discussion of information analysis procedures for determining and financing nonclassroom instruction, Watkins and Ruyle (1979) have noted that in dealing with current credit-hour-based funding formulas, institutions must either adapt the nonclassroom programs' outcome measures to credit-hour equivalents or replace current funding formulas. In determining the cost of a nonclassroom program, they point out that the lower faculty costs are a combination of the design of the program, the age of most programs, and the experience level of the faculty traditionally involved in innovative programs.

The Carnegie Commission (1972) recognizes the potential of nonclassroom programs, especially in the area of technology, to reduce faculty costs. However, they feel that this savings should continue and that by 1990 technology should save 15 percent of a professor's time per course. While acknowledging that technology will require an initial capital investment, the commission predicts that its use will significantly reduce costs in the long run through an increase in productivity. This productivity increase will result from release time for faculty, a longer period during which instruction is available, and the increased interinstitutional sharing of resources and programs. To maximize the return on investment, the commission advises "early investment in areas with the greatest capability for wide use," such as libraries and introductory courses (p. 3).

In their five alternative futures of higher education, Stakenas and Kaufman (1977) identify cost reduction as a benefit of the integration of media into individualized instruction. Again, the savings should result from the elimination of small classes, the computer management of instruction, and a reduction in the number of faculty members. This savings requires a change in orientation from teaching to learning outcomes. Stakenas and Kaufman predict a fifteen- to twenty-year period for cost recovery of the capital outlay for mass methods of instructional technology. This large capital investment often necessitates interinstitutional cooperation in program implementation to effect a quicker cost recovery.

Meeth's (1975) study of funding nontraditional programs indicated that those programs that were parts of traditional public institutions had the most serious problems with funding. These institutions are most closely tied to funding formulas and guidelines based on the academic credit hour: "As a consequence, these programs are often underfunded; thus, they are denied a chance to demonstrate their effectiveness" (p. 178). Meeth lists a number of solutions to this problem, which include passing the costs of the course on to students; grants; political pressure to change the funding formula; the arbitrary assignment of credit hours; the determination of a sum based on full-time student equivalency; developing an outcome-based formula; and program budgeting. He also notes that "goodwill has been an effective substitute for technical solutions" (p. 183), particularly in working with state fiscal agencies.

Student involvement in funding is a major component at both Roger Williams College's University Without Walls Unit and San Francisco's Lone Mountain College. In both colleges, a portion of the student's tuition is rebated so that the student may pay his or her faculty adviser and acquire support materials unique to each learning experience (Tubbs, 1972). The remainder of the tuition pays for the special administrative costs necessitated by the program. These costs include more complex academic records, time for faculty review of students in academic difficulty, and the potential need to contract with businesses or other agencies for special services (Berte, 1975).

Nonclassroom programs have been shown to effect a cost savings for society at large. In 1970 the cost of instruction in nonclassroom programs was $3.00 per enrollee hour, compared to an average instructional cost of $4.13 (Carnegie Commission on Higher Education, 1973).

Evaluation

Chickering (1975) conducted a survey of two hundred and fifty students to determine the effectiveness of learning contracts at Empire State University. Forty-six percent of the students felt that learning contracts were superior to traditional learning methods, and 58 percent felt that learning contracts made a greater contribution to personal development. While 24 percent of the survey respondents saw no weaknesses in the program, 15 percent cited the lack of group interaction as a major weakness. Hodgkinson (1975) notes that "individualized learning requires individualized processes of evaluation" (p. 83). He also indicates that the need for evaluation strategies should be a part of the learning process and thus serve as a diagnostic tool.

Bowen and others (1979) recognize the desire of administrators to protect the integrity of their institutions and not to have their institutions confused with degree factories. In developing an assessment process, questions should be asked to determine each program's ability to respond to the individual needs of students, to determine the characteristics of students in nonclassroom programs, to identify the difficulties in transferring from a classroom to a nonclassroom program, to determine the relationship of program completion to adequate support services, to identify the point in the program at which students experience the most difficulty, to ascertain the value of the program to the student, and to discover the program's impact on the institution's costs.

Angus (1974) describes procedures for program evaluation of experiential education such as questionnaires, longitudinal studies, and the development of inventories such as North Carolina's Internship Style Development Form. Program components that ensure effective evaluation include clearly defined objectives, preexperience orientation, an individualized learning contract and reading list, a written or final report, an examination of cognitive skills gained, post-experience seminars, and self-evaluation. Evaluation practices for student performance could include intermediate feedback, seminars or workshops, critical incident writing, a diary or journal, and an exit interview.

Summary

The literature on nonclassroom learning provides information on the benefits, implementation, costs, and means of assessment. The benefits include the ability to respond to the needs of special learners by greater flexibility in time and place of learning, as well as the orientation of nonclassroom learning to the student's rather than to the institution's needs. A key factor in implementation is the leadership of the initiator. Costs of nonclassroom learning are lower than those of more traditional modes of instruction; however, the credit-hour-based funding formula does not always permit proper funding of these new modes of instruction. Since nonclassroom learning is an individually oriented approach, the process of assessment and evaluation must be concerned with the needs of the individual.

References

Angus, E. L. "Evaluating Experiential Education." In J. Duley (ed.), *Implementing Field Experience Education*. New Directions for Higher Education, no. 6. San Francisco: Jossey-Bass, 1974.
Berte, N. R. (ed.). *Individualizing Education by Learning Contracts*. New Directions for Higher Education, no. 10. San Francisco: Jossey-Bass, 1975.
Bowen, F., Edelstein, S., and Medsker, L. "The Identification of Decision Makers Concerned with Nontraditional Degree Programs and an Analysis of Their Information Needs." In *An Evaluative Look at Nontraditional Post-Secondary Education*. Papers prepared in 1977 by the Center for Research and Development in Higher Education of the University of California, Berkeley. Washington, D.C.: National Institute of Education, 1979.
Carnegie Commission on Higher Education. *The Fourth Revolution: Instructional Technology in Higher Education*. New York: McGraw-Hill, 1972.
Carnegie Commission on Higher Education. *Towards a Learning Society: Alternative Channels to Life, Work, and Service*. New York: McGraw-Hill, 1973.
Carnegie Council on Policy Studies in Higher Education. *Three Thousand Futures: The Next Twenty Years for Higher Education*. San Francisco: Jossey-Bass, 1980.
Chickering, A. W. "Developing Intellectual Competence at Empire State." In N. R. Berte (ed.), *Individualizing Education by Learning Contracts*. New Directions for Higher Education, no. 10. San Francisco: Jossey-Bass, 1975.
Commission on Nontraditional Study. "Recommendations of the Commission." *Chronicle of Higher Education*, 1973, 7 (18), 6.
Dirr, P. J. "Television in Higher Education." In P. J. Tate and M. Kressel (eds.), *The Expanding Role of Telecommunications in Higher Education*. New Directions for Higher Education, no. 44. San Francisco: Jossey-Bass, 1983.
Feeney, J., and Riley, G. "Learning Contracts at New College, Sarasota." In N. R. Berte (ed.), *Individualizing Education by Learning Contracts*. New Directions for Higher Education, no. 10. San Francisco: Jossey-Bass, 1975.
Hodgkinson, H. L. "Evaluating Individualized Learning." In N. R. Berte (ed.), *Individualizing Education by Learning Contracts*. New Direction for Higher Education, no. 10. San Francisco: Jossey-Bass, 1975.
Johnson, S. E. "Faculty Perspectives on Outreach Teaching." *Lifelong Learning*, 1985, 9 (3), 11-14, 28.
Meeth, L. R. "Restrictive Practices in Formula Funding." In D. W. Vermilye (ed.), *Learner-Centered Reform: Current Issues in Higher Education*. San Francisco: Jossey-Bass, 1975.
National Institute of Education. *Involvement in Learning: Realizing the Potential of American Higher Education*. Final report of the Study Group on the Condition of Excellence in American Higher Education. Washington, D.C.: U.S. Government Printing Office, 1984.
O'Connell, W. R., and Moomaw, W. E. "Organizing Innovation: Five Stages." In J. Duley (ed.), *Implementing Field Experience Education*. New Directions for Higher Education, no. 6. San Francisco: Jossey-Bass, 1974.

Quinn, M. E., and Sellars, L. "Role of the Student." In J. Duley (ed.), *Implementing Field Experience Education*. New Directions for Higher Education, no. 6. San Francisco: Jossey-Bass, 1974.

Ramsey, W. R. "Role of the Agency Supervisor." In J. Duley (ed.), *Implementing Field Experience Education*. New Directions for Higher Education, no. 6. San Francisco: Jossey-Bass, 1974.

Stakenas, R. G., and Kaufman, R. A. "Educational Technology and Cost Reduction in Higher Education: Five Alternative Futures." Tallahassee: Florida State University Center for Educational Development and Evaluation, 1977. (ED 169 923)

Stephenson, J. B., and Sexton, R. F. "Institutionalizing Experiential Learning in a State University." In J. Duley (ed.), *Implementing Field Experience Education*. New Directions for Higher Education, no. 6. San Francisco: Jossey-Bass, 1974.

Tate, P. J., and Kressel, M. (eds.). *The Expanding Role of Telecommunications in Higher Education*. New Directions for Higher Education, no. 44. San Francisco: Jossey-Bass, 1983.

Tubbs, W. E. (ed.). *Toward a Community of Seekers: A Report on Experimental Higher Education*. National Symposium on Experimental Higher Education, Johnston College, January 1972. Lincoln: University of Nebraska, Nebraska Curriculum Development Center, 1972.

Van Aalst, F. D. "Program Design." In J. Duley (ed.), *Implementing Field Experience Education*. New Directions for Higher Education, no. 6. San Francisco: Jossey-Bass, 1974.

Watkins, R. W., and Ruyle, J. H. "Information Specifications for Development of Instruments to be Used in the Evaluation of Nontraditional Programs." In *An Evaluative Look at Nontraditional Post-Secondary Education*. Papers prepared in 1977 by the Center for Research and Development in Higher Education of the University of California, Berkeley. Washington, D.C.: National Institute of Education, 1979.

Welling, J. "A Management Perspective." In P. J. Tate and M. Kressel (eds.), *The Expanding Role of Telecommunications in Higher Education*. New Directions for Higher Education, no. 44. San Francisco: Jossey-Bass, 1983.

Jo Ann Carr is director of the School of Education's Instructional Materials Center for the University of Wisconsin–Madison. She is currently chair of the Wisconsin Association of Academic Librarians.

Index

A

Administration: implementation issues for, 11-14; of self-paced instruction, 23-24
Alverno College, and library-based learning, 48
American Association for Higher Education, 1
American Association of Museums, 69
American Society for Engineering Education (ASEE), 40, 44
Angus, E. L., 94, 95
Annenberg, W., 33
Annenberg School of Communications, 28, 30, 31, 33
Arizona, engineers needed in, 37
Arizona State University, Interactive Instructional Television Program (IITP) at, 37, 39, 42, 44
Art galleries. *See* Museums
Association for College Unions International, 83
Astin, A. W., 78, 85, 86
Auraria Library: Library Business Partnership Program of, 54; videotapes by, 50

B

Baack, J., 86
Baier, J. L., 81, 82, 85, 86
Baier, L., 86
Banfield, E., 71, 74
Baskin, S., 1, 5, 8, 15
Beal, P., 85, 86
Bergevin, E. C., 70, 74
Berman, W. F., 78, 86
Berte, N. R., 93, 95
Biedinbach, J. M., 40, 44
Bisesi, M., 37, 40, 44, 45
Bloom, B. S., 18, 25
Bolman, L. G., 8, 10, 15
Borzak, L., 59, 66
Bosco, P. J., 86
Bowen, F., 91, 92, 94, 95
Breivik, P. S., 5, 47, 51, 54, 55
Brey, R., 30, 35
Briggs, L., 18, 25
Brigham Young University, and library-based learning, 50
Brooklyn College, and library-based learning, 51
Brown, R., 81, 86
Bryan, W. T., 82, 86
Burks, D. R., 41, 45

C

Cahn, S. M., 59, 66
California, implementation in, 91
California at Los Angeles, University of, and library-based learning, 50
California at San Diego, University of, and telecourses, 32
Carnegie Commission on Higher Education, 90, 91, 92, 93, 95
Carnegie Council on Policy Studies in Higher Education, 7, 15, 89, 90, 95
Carnegie Foundation for the Advancement of Teaching, 47, 59
Carr, J. A., 3, 4, 89, 96
Carroll, J., 18, 25
Chausow, H. M., 34, 36
Chenette, E. R., 40, 44
Chicago T.V. College, effectiveness of, 34
Chickering, A. W., 40, 44, 59, 66, 94, 95
Coast Community College District, and telecourses, 33
Cohen, P. A., 25
Coleman, J. S., 59, 66
Colorado, library-based learning in, 48
Commission on Museums for a New Century, 70, 74
Commission on Nontraditional Study, 4, 5, 89, 95
Cornell University, and student activities, 85

Corporation for Public Broadcasting, 28, 30, 31, 33
Corporations, and interactive television, 37-45
Costs: of field experience, 65; of interactive television, 41-42; issues of, 3, 12-13; of library-based learning, 53; literature review on, 92-93; of self-paced instruction, 24-25
Cross, K. P., 2, 40, 45, 49, 54
Curtis, D. V., 15

D

Dallas County Community College District, and telecourses, 33
Danels, J., 85
Deal, T. E., 8, 10, 15
Dirr, P. J., 28, 35, 90-91, 95
Downey, R. G., 78, 86
Dunnivant, 89

E

Edelstein, S., 95
Empire State University, learning contracts at, 94
Evaluation: components of, 13-14; of field experience, 64; issues of, 3; literature review on, 94; of museum courses, 73
Eyster, W., 43, 45

F

Faculty: for field experience, 62-63; for interactive television, 43; and library-based learning, 52-53; and self-paced instruction, 19, 20, 22-23
Faculty development, and library-based learning, 53
Federal Communications Commission (FCC), 38
Feeney, J., 91, 95
Felder, B. D., 37, 45
Feldman, K. A., 78, 86
Field experience: activities in, 61-62; advantages of, 58; analysis of, 57-67; background experiences for, 60-61; conclusion on, 66; costs of, 65; credit for, 60; disadvantages of, 58-59; educational value of, 60-62;
evaluation of, 64; faculty for, 62-63; forms of, 57-58; issues in, 65; monitoring, 66; scheduling, 59-60; site identification for, 62; staff for, 63-64; starting, 59
Florida, University of, and interactive television, 38
Froke, M., 28, 36, 41, 45
Fry, R., 59, 66

G

Gagne, R., 18, 25
Georgia Institute of Technology, interactive television at, 38
Glick, D. M., 20, 25
Good, C. V., 17, 25
Greenberg, S., 37, 39, 45
Griffin, G., 41, 45
Grigsby, C., 30, 35

H

Higher education, changing environment for, 7-8
Hodgkinson, H. L., 94, 95
Horton, F. W., Jr., 48, 54

I

Illinois, implementation in, 91
Illinois, University of, interactive television at, 38
Illinois Institute of Technology, interactive television at, 42
Information literacy, 48, 50-51
Ingarden, R., 70, 74
Institutions: climate of, 1, 5, 10-11, 21; and self-paced instruction, 19-20, 21; student activities impact on, 84-86
Instruction, alternative delivery systems for, 2
Instructional Telecommunications Consortium, 30
Instructional Television Fixed Service (ITFS), 32, 38-44
Interactive television: analysis of, 37-45; costs of, 41-42; faculty for, 43; justifications for, 41; need for, 37-38; operation of, 38-39; and quality assurance, 39-41; success factors for, 43-44; summary on, 44

Internships. *See* Field experience
Iowa, University of, student activities at, 82
Iowa State University, interactive television at, 38

J

Johansen, P., 70, 74
Johnson, S. E., 91-92, 95
Julian, A. A., 41, 45

K

Kapfer, M. B., 18, 25
Kapfer, P. G., 18, 25
Katz, J. H., 35
Kaufman, R. A., 93, 96
Keller, F., 18, 19, 23, 24, 25
Kemp, J., 18, 19, 24, 25
Kendall, J. C., 59, 66
Kennedy, A., 10, 15
Kentucky, University of, implementation at, 91
Knapp, P. B., 52, 54
Knox, A. B., 74
Kolb, D. A., 59, 66
Kressel, M., 35, 90-91, 96
Kulik, C. C., 25
Kulik, J. A., 17, 19, 25

L

Laird, D., 15
Lankford, E. L., 71, 75
Lapin, S., 41, 45
Lewis, J. L., 24, 25
Lewis, R. J., 1, 5
Library-based learning: analysis of, 47-55; costs of, 53; developing, 49-52; faculty and, 52-53; and outreach, 53-54; rationale for, 47-49; summary on, 54
Lifelong learning, and nonclassroom learning, 2
Lone Mountain College, funding at, 93

M

McClelland, D. C., 86
McGrath, E. J., 85, 86
Management: administrative issues for, 11-14; analysis of issues in, 7-15; conclusion on, 14; and organizational culture, 10-11; of symbolic issues, 8-10
Mann, R. B., 86
Medsker, L., 95
Meeth, L. R., 93, 95
Meyers, E., 85
Miami-Dade Community College: and library-based learning, 48; and telecourses, 32
Minnesota, University of, interactive television at, 38
Moomaw, W. E., 91, 95
Morrell, R. C., 77, 87
Morrell, S. A., 77, 87
Multiple distribution service (MDS), 38, 41
Munushian, J., 38, 45
Museums: analysis of learning in, 69-75; background on, 69-70; benefits of, 73-74; courses from, 70-72; evaluation of, 73; summary on, 74; and tours abroad, 72-73

N

Naisbitt, J., 12
National Association for Campus Activities, 82, 83
National Association for College and University Residence Halls, 83
National Institute of Education, 90, 95
Nebraska, University of, student activities at, 82
New College, Sarasota, implementation at, 91
New York, implementation in, 91
Newcomb, T. M., 78, 86
Newman, F., 1, 2, 5, 47, 49, 52, 55, 59, 78, 86
Noel, L., 85, 86
Nonclassroom learning: administrative issues for, 11-14; background on, 1-5; budgetary issues of, 12-13; costs and funding of, 92-93; defining, 11-12; evaluation of, 13-14, 94; with field experiences, 57-67; implementation of, 7-15, 91-92; with interactive television, 37-45; library-based, 47-55; literature review for,

Nonclassroom learning *(continued)* 89-96; in museums and art galleries, 69-75; and organizational culture, 10-11; professional and legal issues in, 12; rationale for, 89-91; with self-paced instruction, 17-26; in student activities, 77-87; symbolic issues of, 8-10; with telecourses, 27-36; values and rewards related to, 4
North, R. A., 86
North Carolina, Internship Style Development Form in, 94
North Dakota, implementation in, 91-92
North Dakota, University of, student activities at, 82
Northern Colorado, University of, student activities at, 80

O

O'Connell, W. R., 91, 95
Ohio, interactive television in, 41
Oklahoma State University, interactive television at, 38

P

Patterson, J. A., 69, 75
Pedone, R. J., 35
Pennsylvania State University, telecourses at, 32
Perrin, G., 43, 45
Perry, W., 28, 36
Peterson, R. E., 41, 45
Postlethwait, T. N., 18
Practicums. *See* Field experience
Public Broadcasting Service (PBS), 32, 42; Adult Learning Service (ALS) of, 28, 33
Purdy, L. N., 3, 27, 28, 36

Q

Quality, calls for, 2
Quinn, M. E., 89-90, 96

R

Radzyminski, W., 36
Ramsey, W. R., 91, 96

Reiser, R., 20, 26
Riley, G., 91, 95
Roberts, M. C., 20, 26
Roger Williams College, funding at, 93
Ross-Powers, S. J., 78, 85, 86
Ruyle, J. H., 92, 96

S

St. Cloud University, and student activities, 85
Sanstead, M., 86
Santogrossi, D. A., 20, 26
Schein, E. H., 10, 11, 15
Schramm, W., 28, 36, 43, 45
Schwartz, R., 69, 75
Self-paced instruction: and academic units, 22; administration of, 23-24; advantages of, 18-20; analysis of, 17-26; background on, 17-18; continuing commitment to, 23; costs of, 24-25; defined, 17; development teams for, 22; disadvantages of, 20-21; faculty and, 19, 20, 22-23; fostering, 21-22; summary on, 25; task force for, 21-22
Sellars, L., 89-90, 96
Semb, G., 20, 25
Sexton, R. F., 91, 96
Silver, E. M., 86
Smithsonian Institution, 69
Solinger, J., 69, 75
Southern California, University of: business administration telecourses at, 32; engineering interactive television at, 37-38, 42
Southern California Consortium for Community College Television, 28, 33
Spring, M., 36
Staff: for field experience, 63-64; for interactive television, 43-44; and self-paced instruction, 23; for student activities, 83-84
Stakenas, R. G., 93, 96
Stanford University: interactive television at, 38, 42; telecourses at, 32
Steitz, J. A., 74, 75
Stephenson, J. B., 91, 96
Stewart, A. J., 86

Stowers, M. P., 2, 3, 17, 26
Student activities: analysis of, 77–87; and development transcripts, 81–83; effects of, 77–78; funding issues for, 84; institutional impact of, 84–86; staff for, 83–84; summary on, 86; training methods for, 78–80
Student Development Mentoring-Transcript Clearinghouse, 82
Students: activities participation by, 77–87; competition for, 1–2; and interactive television, 43; and self-paced instruction, 18–19, 20; for telecourses, 30–32
Suput, R. R., 53, 55

T

Tager System, 38
Tate, P. J., 90–91, 96
Telecourses: analysis of, 27–36; conclusion on, 35; effectiveness of, 34–35; information sources on, 28; number and quality of, 32–34; students for, 30–32; and television's impact, 29–30; use of, 27–28
Television: impact of, 2, 3, 29–30; interactive, 37–45; telecourses from, 27–36
Tessmer, M., 2, 3, 17, 26
Texas, interactive television in, 38, 41
Tubbs, W. E., 93, 96

U

Utah, University of, and library-based learning, 50

V

Valery, P., 7
Van Aalst, F. D., 91, 96
Vermont, University of, conference at, 69

W

Walberg, H., 19, 26
Wang, M. C., 19, 26
Wartgow, J. F., 1, 3, 4, 7, 13, 15
Washington, University of, interactive television at, 38
Watkins, R. W., 92, 96
Wayne State University, and Monteith College library-based learning, 52
Welling, J., 90, 96
Williams, M., 85, 86
Winston, R. B., Jr., 85, 86
Winter, D. G., 78, 86
Wisconsin at Parkside, University of, and library-based learning, 50
Witucke, V., 57, 67
Wright, D., 86

Z

Zigerell, J. J., 28, 34, 36
Zuber-Skerritt, O., 28, 36

STATEMENT OF OWNERSHIP, MANAGEMENT AND CIRCULATION

Title of Publication: New Directions for Higher Education
Date of Filing: 9/26/86
Frequency of Issue: Quarterly
No. of Issues Published Annually: 4
Annual Subscription Price: $38 indv/$48 inst

Complete Mailing Address of Known Office of Publication:
433 California St., San Francisco (SF County), CA 94104

Complete Mailing Address of the Headquarters of General Business Offices of the Publisher:
433 California St., San Francisco (SF County), CA 94104

Publisher: Jossey-Bass Inc., Publishers, 433 California St., San Francisco, CA 94104

Editor: Martin Kramer, 2807 Shasta Rd., Berkeley, CA 94708

Owner: Allen Jossey-Bass, Jossey-Bass Publishers, 433 California St., S.F., CA 94104

Known Bondholders, Mortgagees, and Other Security Holders: None

Extent and Nature of Circulation	Avg. No. Copies Each Issue During Preceding 12 Months	Actual No. Copies of Single Issue Published Nearest to Filing Date
	1986	1986
A. Total No. Copies	1588	1655
B. Paid Circulation		
1. Sales through dealers and carriers	204	86
2. Mail Subscription	1828	968
C. Total Paid Circulation	1232	968
D. Free Distribution	87	160
E. Total Distribution	1411	1129
F. Copies Not Distributed	489	527
G. Total	1588	1655

I certify that the statements made by me above are correct and complete.
Vice President